D1622993

How Should the United States Treat Prisoners in the War on Terror?

Other books in the At Issue series:

How Should the United States Treat Prisoners in the War on Terror?

Lauri S. Friedman, *Book Editor*

Bruce Glassman, *Vice President*
Bonnie Szumski, *Publisher*
Helen Cothran, *Managing Editor*

GREENHAVEN PRESS
An imprint of Thomson Gale, a part of The Thomson Corporation

Detroit • New York • San Francisco • San Diego • New Haven, Conn.
Waterville, Maine • London • Munich

LIBRARY OF CONGRESS CATALOGING-IN-PUBLICATION DATA

How should the United States treat prisoners in the war on terror? / Lauri S. Friedman, book editor.
   p. cm. — (At issue)
Includes bibliographical references and index.
ISBN 0-7377-3114-1 (pbk. : alk. paper) — ISBN 0-7377-3113-3 (lib. : alk. paper)
   1. War on terrorism, 2001—Prisoners and prisons, American. 2. Prisoners of war—United States. 3. Prisoners of war—Abuse of—United States. 4. Prisoners of war—Iraq. 5. Prisoners of war—Cuba—Guantánamo Bay Naval Base.
   I. Friedman, Lauri S. II. At issue (San Diego, Calif.)
HV6432.H696 2005
973.931—dc22   2004053501

Contents

Introduction

It is often said that the terrorist attacks of September 11, 2001, marked a turning point in America's history, and that the ensuing war on terror was different from any military endeavor before it. From the outset of the war, President George W. Bush acknowledged the uniqueness of this undertaking. On September 20, 2001, he warned, "This war will not be like [wars before it]. . . . Americans should not expect one battle, but a lengthy campaign unlike any other we have ever seen." Indeed, the war on terror has involved an unprecedented mix of military, diplomatic, financial, and intelligence efforts designed to combat an entirely new kind of enemy. The war on terror has also introduced new problems that have no easy solutions. One such issue is how to deal with prisoners taken during the war.

Any discussion about how to treat prisoners in the war on terror inevitably centers around the Geneva Conventions. During the nineteenth century Western nations began a series of conferences, known as the Geneva Conventions, to formally codify the rules of war. The third of these conferences, held after World War II in 1949, concerned the treatment of prisoners of war. For over half a century the rules established by the Geneva Conventions were regarded as a comprehensive guide for undertaking global conflict. Today's war on terror, however, involves actors not explicitly mentioned in the Geneva Conventions, which were intended to cover traditional wars between nation-states. Therefore, looking to the Geneva Conventions for answers on how to treat prisoners in the war on terror has proven difficult.

At the center of this difficulty is deciding whether the Geneva Conventions are applicable to prisoners taken during the war on terror, many of whom are suspected terrorists. The Geneva Conventions define prisoners of war as soldiers, meaning those who wear the uniform of their nation, have a rank and a superior, fight openly, and avoid violence against civilians at all costs. Terrorists, it is argued, do not wear the uniform of any nation, nor are they part of a traditional army. The Bush administration has thus preferred the term *unlawful combatants* to describe those detained in the war on terror, and it argues that such combatants are not eligible for protection under the Geneva Conventions. Opponents of this argument contend that the detainees are in fact covered under the conventions and that the United States violates international law in denying them the conventions' protection.

The nature of the war on terror—which is being fought to prevent civilian deaths rather than protect territory or other resources, as is the goal of most wars—also contributes to the confusion over how to treat prisoners. When experts talk about how to prevent terrorism and how to treat prisoners in the war on terror, they invariably bring up what is commonly known as the "ticking time bomb theory." In this scenario a suspected terrorist is in custody, and a bomb is about to go off somewhere in the city. Although officials desperately search for the bomb to disarm it, they are nowhere close to finding it and time is running out. The suspect in custody may have information about the location of the bomb, and extracting this information could theoretically save the entire city from destruction. The quandary thus emerges: How far should authorities go to extract such information from the suspect?

Such a predicament seems to have led some U.S. soldiers to abuse prisoners held in Iraq in 2003 and 2004; frustrated by the lack of information they were getting about the deadly insurgency in that country, military personnel stepped up their interrogation methods to include controversial "stress and duress" techniques. These included forcing prisoners into uncomfortable positions for hours at a time, bombarding them with noise and light, and depriving them of sleep for over twenty-four hours. Sometimes interrogators resorted to torture to extract information from suspects. Those in favor of using intensified interrogation methods argue that the information extracted from "stressed" prisoners might save hundreds of lives. As author Tammy Bruce puts it, "I don't care if you put women's underwear on their heads, or frankly, even pull out a few fingernails of those responsible for mass murder, to unmask their continuing plans for the genocide of civilized peoples. . . . It's called 'torture lite,' it works, and I'm all for whatever it takes to get information, and yes, to punish and annihilate terrorist leadership around the world." Those against using such techniques, however, argue that abandoning America's longstanding commitment to human rights endangers Americans in a critical way. On this point international law professor Michael Byers warns, "If human rights are worth anything, they have to apply when governments are most tempted to violate them. . . . Respecting the presumption of POW status and upholding the human rights of detainees today will help to protect our people [who may become detainees in other nations] in the future."

Whether America abides by the Geneva Conventions or creates new regulations, how it chooses to treat its prisoners in the war on terror sets an important example for the rest of the world. Decisions to torture suspects, export them to other countries for violent interrogation, try them by military tribunal, or hold them indefinitely will be duly noted by other countries searching for acceptable ways to combat terrorism.

1

Torturing Prisoners in the War on Terror Is Never Justified

Kenneth Roth

Kenneth Roth is the executive director of Human Rights Watch, a nonprofit organization dedicated to defending human rights around the world.

Torture should never be used to extract information from terrorist suspects. The United States is bound to international treaties and conventions that explicitly prohibit any form of torture. Moreover, suspects who are tortured do not tend to yield accurate or reliable information, as they are likely to say anything simply to make the interrogation end. In addition, because attempts to regulate torture tacitly encourage its use, they only contribute to more mistreatment. Ultimately, the use of torture is morally wrong.

The sexual humiliation of [Iraqi] prisoners [by U.S. soldiers] at Abu Ghraib prison [in Iraq] is so shocking that it risks overshadowing other U.S. interrogation practices that are also reprehensible. And unlike the sexual abuse, these other practices have been sanctioned by the highest levels of government and are probably more widespread.

The Abu Ghraib outrages are not simply the product of a small group of sick and misguided soldiers. They are the predictable result of the Bush administration's policy of permitting "stress and duress" interrogation techniques. The sexual abuse of prisoners, despicable as it is, is a logical consequence of a system put in place after [the terrorist attacks of] Sept. 11, 2001, to ratchet up the pain, discomfort and humiliation of prisoners under interrogation.

"None of These Techniques Is Legal"

The Defense Department has adopted a 72-point "matrix" of types of stress to which detainees can be subjected. These include stripping detainees naked, depriving them of sleep, subjecting them to bright lights or blaring noise, hooding them, exposing them to heat and cold, and binding them in uncomfortable positions. The more stressful techniques must be approved by senior commanders, but all are permitted. And nearly all are being used, according to testimony taken by [the human rights organization] Human Rights Watch from post–Sept. 11 detainees released from U.S. custody.

None of these techniques is legal. Treaties ratified by the United States, including the Geneva Conventions and the U.N. Convention Against Torture, prohibit not only torture but also "cruel, inhuman or degrading treatment or punishment." In ratifying the Convention Against Torture, the U.S. government interpreted this provision to prohibit the same practices as those proscribed by the U.S. Constitution. The Bush administration reiterated that understanding [in] June [2003].

In other words, just as U.S. courts repeatedly have found it unconstitutional for interrogators in American police stations to use these third-degree methods, it is illegal under international law for U.S. interrogators in Iraq, Afghanistan, Guantanamo Bay [Cuba, where terror suspects are held] or elsewhere to employ them. U.S. military manuals ban these "stress and duress" techniques, and federal law condemns them as war crimes. Yet the Bush administration has authorized them.

Torture Is Always Wrong

But doesn't the extraordinary threat of terrorism demand this extraordinary response? No. The prohibition of torture and cruel, inhuman, or degrading treatment or punishment is absolute and unconditional, in peace or in war. This dehumanizing practice is always wrong.

Moreover, resorting to abusive interrogation is counterproductive. People under torture will say anything, true or not. And whatever marginal advantage interrogators might gain by applying these techniques is vastly outweighed by the global disgust at American use of them. Coupled with anger at other lawless practices, such as the Bush administration's refusal to apply the Geneva Conventions to the Guantanamo detainees,[1] that revulsion has contributed to America's plummeting esteem. Allies are less willing to cooperate in combating terrorism, and terrorist recruiters must be having a field day.

> *" People under torture will say anything, true or not. "*

But can't torture at least be used on someone who might know of an imminent terrorist act? Not without opening the door to pervasive torture. The problem with this "ticking bomb" scenario is that it is infinitely elastic. Why stop with the terrorist suspect himself? Why not torture his neighbor or friend who might know something about an attack? And why stop with an imminent attack? Aren't the potential victims of possible future attacks just as worthy of protection by torture? The slope is very slippery.

Regulating Torture Only Encourages It

It has been argued that because some interrogators will inevitably resort to coercion, torture should be regulated. But by signaling that torture and mistreatment are sometimes justified, regulation ends up encouraging more Abu Ghraibs.

Government officials are also notoriously poor at regulating coercive interrogation techniques. For example, Israel's effort to regulate the application of "moderate physical pressure" led to deaths in custody and ultimately a decision by Israel's Supreme Court to outlaw it. Human Rights Watch and others have repeatedly reported abusive techniques on the part of U.S. interrogators, but the Bush administration did nothing to address them until the photographs of Abu Ghraib became public. In-

1. The author refers to the controversy over status of the detainees held at Guantanamo Bay, Cuba. The Bush administration argues that the detainees should be designated as "enemy combatants" because they fought for no particular country; this exempts them from the rights of prisoners of war protected by the Geneva Convention.

deed, to this day, no one has been prosecuted for two deaths of detainees in U.S. custody in Afghanistan; medical examiners declared those deaths "homicides" a year and a half ago.

Maj. Gen. Geoffrey D. Miller announced last week [May 2004] that certain stress interrogation techniques will no longer be used in Iraq. That's a useful first step. President Bush should now ban all forms of "stress and duress" interrogation, in Iraq and elsewhere. Various noncoercive methods, from inducements to trickery, can still be used, as able interrogators have done for decades. And no one contends that detention centers should be country clubs. But the deliberate ratcheting up of pain, suffering and humiliation as an interrogation technique must be stopped. It is wrong itself, and it leads to further atrocities.

2

Torture Should Be Legalized So It Can Be Regulated

Alan M. Dershowitz

A law professor at Harvard University, Alan M. Dershowitz is the author of Why Terrorism Works.

There is much debate over whether it is ever justified to use torture to extract potentially lifesaving information from people reluctant to talk. Although torture is publicly condemned, it is often used surreptitiously by government officials who seek information from suspected terrorists who may know about future terrorist attacks. Such stealthy operations are conducted outside the law and thus are not subject to examination. Torture should therefore be legalized so it can be regulated and controlled. If torture is legalized but subject to the rules of law, officials can get valuable information from suspects and at the same time safeguard the rights of defendants.

The FBI's frustration over its inability to get material witnesses [that is, terror suspects] to talk has raised a disturbing question rarely debated in this country: When, if ever, is it justified to resort to unconventional techniques such as truth serum, moderate physical pressure and outright torture?

The U.S. Constitution Does Not Prohibit Torture

The constitutional answer to this question may surprise people who are not familiar with the current U.S. Supreme Court interpretation of the 5th Amendment privilege against self-incrimination[1]: Any interrogation technique, including the use of truth serum or even torture, is not prohibited. All that is prohibited is the introduction into evidence of the fruits of such techniques in a criminal trial against the person on whom the techniques were used. But the evidence could be used against that suspect in a non-criminal case—such as a deportation hearing—or against someone else.

If a suspect is given "use immunity"—a judicial decree announcing in advance that nothing the defendant says (or its fruits) can be used against him in a criminal case—he can be compelled to answer all proper questions.[2] The issue then becomes what sorts of pressures can constitutionally be used to implement that compulsion. We know that he can be imprisoned until he talks. But what if imprisonment is insufficient to compel him to do what he has a legal obligation to do? Can other techniques of compulsion be attempted?

Exploring the Legality of Truth Serum

Let's start with truth serum. What right would be violated if an immunized suspect [that is, one who has been granted immunity] who refused to comply with his legal obligation to answer questions truthfully were compelled to submit to an injection that made him do so? Not his privilege against self-incrimination, since he has no such privilege now that he has been given immunity.

> *If we are to have torture, it should be authorized by the law.*

What about his right of bodily integrity? The involuntariness of the injection itself does not pose a constitutional barrier. No less a civil libertarian than Justice William J. Brennan rendered a decision that permitted an allegedly drunken driver to

---

1. That is, a person's right to not testify against themselves, commonly called "pleading the fifth."   2. Immunity is frequently given to defendants who possess valuable information but refuse to talk for fear of being punished. Upon receiving immunity status, they cannot be punished for their crimes, but are obligated to reveal all relevant information.

be involuntarily injected to remove blood for alcohol testing. Certainly there can be no constitutional distinction between an injection that removes a liquid and one that injects a liquid.

What about the nature of the substance injected? If it is relatively benign and creates no significant health risk, the only issue would be that it compels the recipient to do something he doesn't want to do. But he has a legal obligation to do precisely what the serum compels him to do: answer all questions truthfully.

Occasions to Consider Torture

What if the truth serum doesn't work? Could the judge issue a "torture warrant," authorizing the FBI to employ specified forms of non-lethal physical pressure to compel the immunized suspect to talk?

> *Judges should have to issue a 'torture warrant' in each case. Thus we would not be winking an eye of quiet approval at torture while publicly condemning it.*

Here we run into another provision of the Constitution— the due process clause,[3] which may include a general "shock the conscience" test. And torture in general certainly shocks the conscience of most civilized nations. But what if it were limited to the rare "ticking bomb" case—the situation in which a captured terrorist who knows of an imminent large-scale threat refuses to disclose it?

Would torturing one guilty terrorist to prevent the deaths of a thousand innocent civilians shock the conscience of all decent people?

To prove that it would not, consider a situation in which a kidnapped child had been buried in a box with two hours of oxygen. The kidnapper refuses to disclose its location. Should we not consider torture in that situation? . . .

All of that said, the argument for allowing torture as an ap-

---

3. Due process is the established course for judicial proceedings designed to safeguard the legal rights of individuals.

proved technique, even in a narrowly specified range of cases, is very troubling.

Torture Should Be Legalized and Regulated

We know from experience that law enforcement personnel who are given limited authority to torture will expand its use. The cases that have generated the current debate over torture illustrate this problem. And, concerning the arrests made following the September 11 [2001 terrorist] attacks, there is no reason to believe that the detainees know about specific future terrorist targets. Yet there have been calls to torture these detainees.

I have no doubt that if an actual ticking bomb situation were to arise, our law enforcement authorities would torture. The real debate is whether such torture should take place outside of our legal system or within it. The answer to this seems clear: If we are to have torture, it should be authorized by the law.

Judges should have to issue a "torture warrant" in each case. Thus we would not be winking an eye of quiet approval at torture while publicly condemning it.

Democracy requires accountability and transparency, especially when extraordinary steps are taken. Most important, it requires compliance with the rule of law. And such compliance is impossible when an extraordinary technique, such as torture, operates outside of the law.

3

America Treats Its Prisoners of War Better than the Arab World Does

Frida Ghitis

Journalist Frida Ghitis is the author of The End of Revolution: A Changing World in the Age of Live Television.

Despite revelations of prisoner abuse by American soldiers in Iraq in 2004, the United States treats its prisoners of war better than the governments of the Arab world. Saudi Arabia, Egypt, Syria, and Sudan are notorious for torturing and murdering their prisoners. The outrage they express over the abuse of prisoners at American hands is therefore ridiculous and hypocritical. Although they are trying to cast blame on the United States in order to shift their citizens' attention away from problems at home, in criticizing American prisoner abuse they only further spotlight their own crimes on the world stage.

Revulsion at the revelations of prisoner abuse by American forces in Iraq[1] has spread faster than hot sand in the dry

1. In the spring of 2004 it came to light that abuses had been committed in the American-controlled Iraqi detention facility known as Abu Ghraib. Photographs surfaced showing U.S. soldiers cheerfully posing beside Iraqi prisoners who had been stripped naked and forced into uncomfortable positions or stacked in piles. Other photographs showed naked Iraqis being attacked by police dogs and otherwise terrorized or humiliated.

desert wind. No one has expressed the outrage with more horror than the American people. No one, that is, except the leaders of the Arab world.

Arab Leaders Are Hypocrites

Both Americans and Arabs are fully justified in their disgust. Yet the reactions of some Arab leaders might qualify as humorous if the deeds of the jailers were not so sickening and their consequences so disastrous. Indeed, some of those expressing shock and horror at the very thought of prisoner mistreatment are governments whose use of torture is routine in countries where human rights organizations have repeatedly reported the torture of prisoners is "endemic" and "widespread."

Should the United States be held to a higher standard? You bet. This is one case where the double standard is justified because the United States entered Iraq on a mission deliberately hued with high moral goals.

> *Some of those expressing shock and horror at the very thought of prisoner mistreatment are governments whose use of torture is routine.*

And yet when dictatorships that have stayed in power for decades declare themselves shocked—shocked!—at the mere idea that a prisoner might be mistreated, there is little question that the outrage is little more than a hollow pantomime. The charade by these suddenly incensed regimes follows a familiar script: Find someone outside the regime to blame and turn the populations' attention away from the problems at home, thereby turning domestic rage away from the oppressive regime.

Prisoner Torture Is Common Throughout the Middle East

Throughout the Arab world, from Saudi Arabia to Egypt and Syria—countries where a call for democracy can land you in jail—government officials and regime-controlled newspapers have spoken of their deep disgust at what they have seen.

Amr Mousa, the secretary-general of the Arab League and

former foreign minister of Egypt, declared his "shock and disgust" at the "shameful images" of the naked prisoners. Shock and disgust somehow eluded him during his many years of service to a dictatorship that tortures opponents of the regime, according to reports of major international human rights organizations. Some of the people subjected to detention and brutal beatings last year [2003], as documented by Human Rights Watch and others, were opponents of the war in Iraq.

> *Condemnation of the Iraqi prisoner abuses came from none other than the Arab-dominated government of Sudan, a genocidal regime that has made killing its own citizens state policy.*

Perhaps it was the Iraqi victims' nakedness that, as we are repeatedly told, has brought so much consternation to the sensitivities of the Arab people. To be sure, there are cultural differences between the Arab world and the West: According to Human Rights Watch, for example, homosexual men have been entrapped, arrested and tortured by Egyptian security forces.

Syrian government newspapers also expressed horror at the mistreatment of Iraqi prisoners. This from a country with a decades-old dictatorship that has killed thousands upon thousands of its citizens and where, [in 2004], a local group reported that political prisoners in government custody suffer unspeakable treatment that often leads to serious injury or death.

At the United Nations, condemnation of the Iraqi prisoner abuses came from none other than the Arab-dominated government of Sudan, a genocidal regime that has made killing its own citizens state policy, slaughtering Christians in the South and aiding in massacres of non-Arab Muslims in the West.

Highlighting Their Own Violations

Torture of prisoners is hardly shocking in many Arab countries, no matter what leaders with a newfound love for human rights now proclaim. In fact, the same governments that today so deeply feel the suffering of Iraqi prisoners found little to complain about in the grotesque abuses of [former Iraqi dictator] Saddam Hussein's regime. The techniques that left hundreds of thousands of Iraqis in mass graves and kept torture chambers stained with human blood did not cause much consternation among Arab leaders.

We hold Western democracies to humanitarian and democratic principles, as we should. But regimes that use torture as a normal part of their efforts to keep their stranglehold in power, as do many in the Middle East, are highlighting their own violations by speaking out against the outrages at Abu Ghraib.

They should speak up, surely. And later, when the storm over Iraq quiets, they should examine their words as closely as their own people will.

4

America Treats Its Prisoners of War Worse than the Arab World Does

Charles Glass

Charles Glass is an international correspondent for CNN and Time. *He has written two books,* Tribes with Flags *and* Money for Old Rope.

Although the U.S. Constitution prohibits cruel and unusual punishment, the prisoners held in the war on terror are being treated inhumanely. In fact, American-held prisoners of war are treated worse than prisoners held by the terrorist group Hezbollah in the 1980s. The detainees at the American detention facility in Guantánamo Bay, Cuba, are subject to conditions that violate the Geneva Conventions, which stipulate how prisoners of war must be treated. Because the United States does not consider combatants in the war on terror to be prisoners of war, it believes it is not required to follow the international regulations. The United States must hold itself to higher standards of ethical treatment, like those set forth in its most treasured document, the Bill of Rights.

The first thing they do is cover your eyes. They make you strip to make sure you're not carrying anything. They replace your clothes with uniforms that are not clothes at all. They chain you by hand and foot. They drag you away and

Charles Glass, "I Know What Camp X-Ray Feels Like: Charles Glass on How His Fellow Americans Treat Prisoners Worse than Hezbollah Treated Him," *New Statesman*, vol. 131, January 28, 2002, p. 12. Copyright © 2002 by New Statesman, Ltd. Reproduced by permission.

leave you on your own. They interrogate you. They say you are going to die if you won't talk. They feed you—you're not much good to them if you starve to death.

It sounds like Camp X-Ray in Guantanamo Bay, Cuba, to which the United States military is deporting men it has captured in Afghanistan.[1] But it was Lebanon in the 1980s. The [terrorist group] Hezbollah, Lebanon's Shi'ite Muslim Party of God, kidnapped foreigners between 1982 and 1989 at the behest of their Iranian benefactors. I remember the drill—the blindfold, chains, solitude and loneliness. I was there for two months in 1987. It was a bad time, and it seemed unlikely to me then that I would one day see photographs of my countrymen treating Muslim prisoners much as I was treated.

The Bill of Rights Is Supposed to Apply to All

I thought the Eighth Amendment to the US constitution prohibited "cruel and unusual punishments". I'm looking at the Bill of Rights, the first ten amendments that Americans regard as sacred, and read the words "nor cruel and unusual punishments inflicted". Full stop. It does not say that only American passport-holders, legal residents of the United States and members of the Senate who take contributions from corporations that violate the law are exempt from government torments. It makes clear that no category of human being is excluded from America's obligation to refrain from cruel and unusual punishments. Amendment VIII means suspects; it means enemies; it means criminals; it means prisoners of war; it means—and the term is as new to me and you as it undoubtedly is to the US defence secretary, Donald Rumsfeld—"illegal" combatants. Who is illegal and who is legal, by the way, has always been for the courts of the United States to decide, not the Department of Defence. As for international law, the Geneva Conventions[2] say that "captured combatants or civilians" have certain rights—including to correspond with their families—without any distinction between "legal" and "illegal" combatants.

I wonder now whether some mullah [a Shi'ite religious

---

1. In October 2001 the United States invaded Afghanistan for sheltering the terrorist group al Qaeda. Hundreds of Afghan fighters who supported al Qaeda and Afghanistan's Taliban government were captured and sent to the U.S. military detention center in Cuba, where they are being held indefinitely.   2. The Geneva Conventions contain internationally recognized standards for the proper conduct of war and the ethical treatment of prisoners of war.

leader] in Tehran [Iran] said, when a score of Americans and Europeans were illegally held against their will in Lebanon: "Obviously, anyone would be concerned if people were suggesting that treatment was not proper." That is what Rumsfeld said on television the other day. Rumsfeld's concern for the Muslims chained like [the Shakespearean beast] Caliban on America's Caribbean base seems to match what Tehran's mullahs felt for us. The mullahs, at least, knew that holding American, French, British and German captives in Lebanon during the 1980s was so shameful that they never admitted it. Rumsfeld seems proud. His is not some secret operation, like the CIA's Phoenix programme of assassinations and torture in Vietnam. It's out in the open.

Hezbollah Treats Its Prisoners Better than America Does

If Rumsfeld has not read the constitution to which he has taken an oath, if he does not see the cruelty in the treatment of those men in Cuba, he could at least admit that tying men up, blocking their sight, cutting them off from their families and flying them around the world is unusual.

"The fact is that treatment is proper," Rumsfeld insisted. "There is no doubt in my mind that it is humane and appropriate and consistent with the Geneva Conventions for the most part." For the most part? Which part? The shackles? The blindfold goggles? The six-by-eight-foot cages? At least Hezbollah put me in a normal-sized room.

> *[Hezbollah turned] the electric lights off at night so I could sleep. The men in Guantanamo enjoy no such luxury.*

It wasn't much of a room, bare but for a paper-thin mattress on the floor, with a sheet of steel to seal the window. I never saw daylight, but they did turn the electric lights off at night so I could sleep. The men in Guantanamo enjoy no such luxury: lights are left on all night so the US marine guards can keep an eye on them. I'm not sure why. Where are they going to go? We are told they don't even know where they are. If they manage to clear the fences and minefields, the Cubans on the other side have said they'll hand them back to the US.

During the 62 days I spent alone in that room in Beirut, all I could do was sit for hours and hours, thinking, praying, hoping. Some friends of mine did that for five years. It was mistreatment, cruel and unusual. The Hezbollah interrogators justified it. The Israeli army, they said, kept Lebanese inmates of Khiam prison, in south Lebanon, under worse conditions. (When international observers at last went into Khiam after Israel's withdrawal from Lebanon in 2000, they confirmed that the interrogation rooms and cells were much, much worse than anything I had experienced as a hostage.) The Israelis' brutality to their prisoners no more justified what the Hezbollah did to its hostages in Lebanon than the Hezbollah's actions excuse what the US is doing in Cuba.

Rumsfeld Should Wear a Hood

An American may some day be arrested or kidnapped by those whose sympathies lie with the Camp X-Ray detainees. What will his captors say when he pleads that his conditions violate international law? Will their answer be to play for him videotapes of the X-Ray detainees and of Rumsfeld's press conferences?

Britain, as it has done with every US action in every battle or bombardment for the past 20 years, justified Camp X-Ray. A government spokesman was quoted as saying, after a British delegation toured the camp last Friday: "There were no gags, no goggles, no earmuffs and no shackles while the detainees were in their cells."

Why would anyone need to shackle and blind them in their cells? The Hezbollah let its hostages remove their blindfolds when they were alone in their locked rooms. When a guard or interrogator entered, however, the blindfold had to come on quickly. The Hezbollahi, realising that they might be held accountable in court for their crimes, did not want us to identify them. It was a sensible precaution. Perhaps Rumsfeld should wear a hood over his head so no one will recognise him.

5

Mistreating Prisoners of War Puts American Soldiers at Risk

Lawrence J. Korb and John Halpin

Lawrence J. Korb was the assistant secretary of defense in the Reagan administration. He is currently a senior fellow at the Center for American Progress, where John Halpin is director of research.

The U.S. government's failure to respond to early reports of prisoner abuse in Iraqi detention facilities in 2003 and 2004 has threatened the lives of American soldiers serving in the Middle East. U.S. soldiers will experience heightened resistance to the occupation of Iraq, and Americans who are captured can expect to be tortured and abused. Revelations of prisoner abuse has also damaged America's reputation abroad, and terrorists will use the images of U.S. soldiers abusing Iraqis to recruit more terrorists to their cause. The Bush administration's failure to adequately address the prisoner abuse scandal has tarnished American credibility and impeded the war on terror.

The horrific pictures of U.S. soldiers abusing Iraqi prisoners at Abu Ghraib[1]—Saddam Hussein's infamous torture chamber—sadden and infuriate all Americans.

While these revelations have exploded on the world stage

---

1. In the spring of 2004 it came to light that terrible abuses had been committed in the American-controlled Iraqi detention facility known as Abu Ghraib.

Lawrence J. Korb and John Halpin, "Cover-Up of Abu Ghraib Torture Put Troops at Risk," www.americanprogress.org, May 11, 2004. This material was created by the Center for American Progress. Reproduced by permission.

and are likely to worsen as new evidence emerges, it is now clear that senior military and Bush administration officials did not adequately train the soldiers and civilian contractors assigned to the prison and were aware of alleged prison abuses in Iraq as early as November 2003.

Senior officials did nothing either to deal with the charges when they emerged or to strategically plan for the explosive fallout the images have produced around the globe, especially in the Arab world. This failure to deal immediately and decisively with these allegations goes all the way to the top. It is a severe dereliction of duty that has unnecessarily exposed U.S. fighting men and women to increased danger in Iraq, increased the probability of terrorist attacks against Americans, and further harmed America's image abroad.

Torture Scandal Will Harm War Effort

Some are already comparing Abu Ghraib to the My Lai massacre during the Vietnam War where more than 500 innocent civilians were killed by American troops on the morning of March 16, 1968. On the surface, the allegations at Abu Ghraib appear less serious, although equally disturbing.

But like My Lai, the real story of Abu Ghraib lies in the potential cover-up of human rights abuses, the lack of adequate training for military personnel, the failure of senior American military and government officials to conduct a swift and thorough public investigation, and the failure to prepare for the sweeping impact the allegations had in the court of world opinion.

It took more than a year for the full story of My Lai to surface. When it did, American support for the Vietnam War—already shaken by the Tet Offensive[2]—took a dramatic turn for the worse and the reputations of the U.S. military and government were irreparably harmed.

We are likely to see a similar conclusion to the Abu Ghraib situation.

We now know that Major General Antonio Taguba produced a 53-page report detailing alleged torture in Abu Ghraib for Lieutenant General Ricardo Sanchez, senior commander in

2. At the height of the Vietnam War in 1968, North Vietnamese forces launched a surprise attack against the south called the Tet Offensive. Although American forces eventually fended off the attackers, the Tet Offensive revealed the weakness of the U.S. military and is remembered as a turning point in the Vietnam War.

Iraq. Sanchez received this report in February 2004—two months before the first graphic photos of abuses were shown publicly on [the television news program] *60 Minutes II.*

Taguba's report documents numerous instances of "sadistic, blatant, and wanton criminal abuses at Abu Ghraib" dating from October to December 2003.

More damaging, three months before Taguba's report was produced, Major General Donald Ryder filed a similar warning of potential human rights violations in Iraqi prisons and in Afghanistan [during the U.S. war there in 2001]. And the International Committee of the Red Cross has been warning the Bush administration of these same problems for more than a year.

It is now clear senior military and administration officials—including General Sanchez, Chairman of the Joint Chiefs of Staff Richard Myers, Secretary of Defense [Donald] Rumsfeld, and President [George W.] Bush—were aware, or should have been aware, months ago that serious problems existed in how American service members were treating enemy soldiers in Iraq.

> *It is a severe dereliction of duty that has unnecessarily exposed U.S. fighting men and women to increased danger in Iraq . . . and further harmed America's image abroad.*

Despite these early warnings—and the potential explosiveness of torture allegations in Iraq and across the Middle East—the Bush administration and U.S. military commanders did nothing to aggressively investigate and punish offenders and had no plan to deal with the fallout.

Their strategy for handling public reactions here and in the Middle East amounted to little more than asking CBS News to forego publishing the graphic photos of torture and humiliation.

When the photos were published everyone from President Bush to General Myers appeared dumbfounded. On May 2, 2004, three weeks after becoming aware that CBS had the photos, General Myers amazingly claimed he had not read the Taguba report, saying, "It's working its way to me." Secretary Rumsfeld as well stated he had not read the full report even days after the photos first aired on television.

American Troops Are in Grave Danger

At a time when U.S. troops were facing rising violence in Iraq, the failure to deal with these explosive charges immediately and decisively violates the tenets of leadership and places our soldiers on the ground, and other Americans in the Middle East, in severe danger—an unjustifiable neglect of duty under any scenario.

> *More Iraqis and Arabs in the Middle East will rise up and fight harder against the perceived injustices and hypocrisy of American forces occupying the region.*

The dangers include:
- More Iraqis and Arabs in the Middle East will rise up and fight harder against the perceived injustices and hypocrisy of American forces occupying the region.
- American soldiers captured in the future will be at greater risk for similar torture and abuse.
- Diplomatic efforts to repair America's image and restore confidence in our motives and intentions will be hindered or worse, viewed as disingenuous.
- [Terrorist leader] Osama bin Laden will use the alleged abuses and potential cover-up to recruit new terrorists for generations.
- The peace in Iraq may be permanently lost and the war on terrorism set back for years.

President Bush and senior military commanders assure us that the perpetrators of these abuses will be fully investigated and punished for their actions. But disciplining some lower ranking military personnel is not enough. While we must wait for the full details to emerge, it is difficult to avoid concluding that the failures extend all the way to the top.

Restoring America's Credibility

The highest levels of the U.S. military, the Defense Department, and the White House must be held accountable for putting our troops at greater risk and diminishing America's moral authority across the globe. As widely discussed . . . , resignations of senior officials, up to and including the Secretary of Defense, should be in order.

Beyond accountability, all remaining pictures and evidence should be released as soon as possible; the U.S.-administered prison system in Iraq must be opened to international inspection immediately; an international Permanent Committee for Monitoring Prison Conditions should be established to formally oversee the prison system in Iraq; and the new Iraqi Ministry of Interior should establish a citizen's liaison to compile and keep a centralized database of all detainees in prisons so Iraqis can locate their families.

America's long-term credibility is on the line. President Bush must do everything possible at this point to restore trust, ensure transparency, and prove to the world that America truly is a beacon for democracy and freedom.

6

Americans Overreact to Reports of Prisoner Abuse

Mortimer B. Zuckerman

Mortimer B. Zuckerman is the editor-in-chief of U.S. News & World Report. *He is also chairman and copublisher of the* New York Daily News.

Americans and the American news media have overreacted to reports of prisoner mistreatment in Iraq. While photos of U.S. soldiers abusing Iraqi prisoners are disturbing, they are not as bad as reports of prison torture and mistreatment in other parts of the world. Moreover, although the prisoner abuses represent a setback for a nation that touts itself as a champion of human rights, America has taken impressive steps to correct its mistake. Even prior to the public release of the photos, the U.S. military began investigating those soldiers responsible, a testament to the openness and accountability inherent in American democracy. Contempt and outrage should thus be reserved for countries in the world that practice mass murder and commit serious torture offenses.

The video of the beheading of Nicholas Berg[1] adds yet another layer of horror and cruelty to the record of Islamic fanatics. "Pure Evil," headlined the *New York Daily News;* "Prisoner Abuse,

1. Nicholas Berg was a private contractor working on rebuilding Iraq after the 2003 war. In May 2004 he was captured and beheaded by Iraqi insurgents who sought revenge for the prisoner abuses committed by U.S. soldiers at Abu Ghraib prison.

Mortimer B. Zuckerman, "A Bit of Perspective, Please," *U.S. News & World Report*, vol. 136, May 24, 2004, p. 68. Copyright © 2004 by U.S. News & World Report, LP. All rights reserved. Reproduced with permission.

Iraqi Style," wrote the *Boston Herald*. It reveals a culture in which "hatred trumps bread," to use [author] Cynthia Ozick's phrase from the *Wall Street Journal*. A culture that glories in the death of innocents thus makes clear whom we are fighting and why. We are up against people who are incited to suppress the most basic human instinct, which is to live, and are willing to kill themselves in their efforts to destroy as many innocent civilians as they can. Our culture, which celebrates life, is utterly mystified.

> ❝ *Let us then not go overboard in our revulsion at the Iraq prison abuses.* ❞

Let us then not go overboard in our revulsion at the Iraq prison abuses.[2] The photographs have been broadcast endlessly in Arab media and denounced from every minaret, but the reaction on the street has been mild—milder than here! The photos offend Arab sensibilities, just as they offend ours. But in virtually every Muslim country, from Morocco to Pakistan, the people know that their prisons systematically practice real torture—and even murder—and that their autocratic leaderships visit barbarity on their own people as a matter of everyday routine.

A Hypocritical Rage

Hypocrisy. [Former Iraqi dictator] Saddam Hussein was a mass murderer. Syria's Hafez Assad wiped out more than 10,000 of his own citizens in Hama in a few days. Jordan's King Hussein broke the Abu Nidal terrorist gang by threatening their members (a threat on occasion carried out) with the murder of their mothers; it worked. Egypt has endured decades of emergency rule and what a recent Human Rights Watch report characterized as a "torture epidemic." Then there is the Saudi royal family, global financier of Muslim religious extremists, whose de facto ruler, Crown Prince Abdullah, blamed the terrorism now infecting his kingdom on the Zionists [pro-Israel political activists] and whose interior minister blamed [the September 11,

2. In the spring of 2004 it came to light that terrible abuses had been committed in at least one American-controlled Iraqi detention facility. Prisoners were sexually humiliated, physically abused, and psychologically terrorized by U.S. soldiers.

2001, terrorist attacks] on Jews. Never mind the Palestinians, whose major gift to mankind is ever new forms of terrorism and whose Hamas [a terrorist group] members reportedly decapitated an Israeli soldier and played football with his head.

The Arab media did attack a government as depraved, brutal, and "satanic." It was, alas, the United States. The hypocrisy is transparent. Arab media elites know full well what American values are, but they simulate rage because that's the prudent thing to do in autocracies that survive by focusing internal resentment on externals, like America, the West, and Israel.

> **"** *It is said that the images from Abu Ghraib blur the moral difference between America and Saddam Hussein. This reflects the moral obtuseness of those who say such things.* **"**

It is said that the images from Abu Ghraib blur the moral difference between America and Saddam Hussein. This reflects the moral obtuseness of those who say such things. Moral obtuseness, of course, is an art form for many in Europe, who consistently ignore the crimes of terrorists. Such people, in the words of [philosopher] Raymond Aron, are "merciless toward the failings of the democracies but ready to tolerate the worst crimes, as long as they are committed in the name of the proper doctrine."

None of this is to excuse what happened at Abu Ghraib. It has stained our high moral purpose. It is no defense to say that the offenders were just a benighted few or were seeking valuable intelligence, or even that torture is prevalent throughout the Arab world. We hold ourselves to a different standard. [U.S. Secretary of Defense] Donald Rumsfeld acted in this tradition when he went before Congress and held himself accountable as a civilian leader in a civilized society.

Do Not Overlook the Facts

In all the furor over the photographs from Abu Ghraib, what's been overlooked by many is the fact that the American military was not only already investigating allegations but announced that the inquiry had begun [in early 2004]. Maj. Gen. Antonio Taguba's investigation was thorough, and his conclusion was that the abuse was the result of the actions of a handful of guards and their superiors, not the result of an official policy or order.

What turned a smoldering investigation into a media firestorm, of course, were the photos. But once again the American public has kept perspective better than the news media. In two polls, a *Washington Post*/ABC and a CNN/*USA Today*/Gallup poll, roughly 70 percent reject any move to oust Rumsfeld, recognizing that it would be an implicit admission that a central thrust of the war against terrorism has been a failure. Rumsfeld should remain: He is a uniquely gifted secretary of defense.[3]

President Bush's critics seek to use Rumsfeld as a pinata and this scandal as a chance to discredit the entire Iraqi venture. But we must not lose faith. The murder of Nick Berg underscores the stakes. Our enemies will never understand America and its values, but they would surely recognize weakness, if we ever allowed them to see it.

3. Donald Rumsfeld was not removed from office.

7

Americans Have Been Humiliated by Reports of Prisoner Abuse

Al Gore

Al Gore was the vice president of the United States from 1992 to 2000.

The war in Iraq, the indefinite detention of combatants in undisclosed military locations, and the revelation of prisoner abuse at the hands of American soldiers has tarnished America's role as an international moral leader. The abuse of prisoners was the natural consequence of the flawed and immoral policies pursued by U.S. government officials, who should ultimately be held accountable for these atrocities. All Americans—soldiers and civilians—have been humiliated by America's follies during the war on terrorism. In dishonoring the rule of law, justice, and freedom that the nation traditionally embodies, the Bush administration has dishonored the United States of America.

[P]resident] George W. Bush promised us a foreign policy with humility. Instead, he has brought us humiliation in the eyes of the world.

He promised to "restore honor and integrity to the White House." Instead, he has brought deep dishonor to our country and built a durable reputation as the most dishonest president since Richard Nixon.

Honor? He decided not to honor the Geneva Convention.[1] Just as he would not honor the United Nations, international treaties, the opinions of our allies, the role of Congress and the courts, or what [former president Thomas] Jefferson described as "a decent respect for the opinion of mankind." He did not honor the advice, experience and judgment of our military leaders in designing his invasion of Iraq [in 2003]. And now he will not honor our fallen dead by attending any funerals or even by permitting photos of their flag-draped coffins.

How did we get from September 12th, 2001, when a leading French newspaper ran a giant headline with the words "We Are All Americans Now" [in honor of the terrorist attacks of September 11, 2001] and when we had the good will and empathy of all the world—to the horror that we all felt in witnessing the pictures of torture in Abu Ghraib?[2] . . .

What happened at the prison, it is now clear, was not the result of random acts by "a few bad apples," it was the natural consequence of the Bush Administration policy that has dismantled those wise constraints and has made war on America's checks and balances.

The abuse of the prisoners at Abu Ghraib flowed directly from the abuse of the truth that characterized the Administration's march to war and the abuse of the trust that had been placed in President Bush by the American people in the aftermath of September 11th.

"On the Brink of Failure"

There was then, there is now and there would have been regardless of what Bush did, a threat of terrorism that we would have to deal with. But instead of making it better, he has made it infinitely worse. We are less safe because of his policies. He has created more anger and righteous indignation against us as Americans than any leader of our country in the 228 years of our existence as a nation—because of his attitude of contempt for any person, institution or nation who disagrees with him.

1. The Geneva Convention contains internationally recognized standards for the proper conduct of war and the ethical treatment of prisoners of war.   2. In the spring of 2004 it came to light that abuses had been committed in the American-controlled Iraqi detention facility known as Abu Ghraib. Photographs surfaced showing U.S. soldiers cheerfully posing beside Iraqi prisoners who had been stripped naked and forced into uncomfortable positions or stacked in piles. Other photographs showed naked Iraqis being attacked by police dogs and otherwise terrorized or humiliated.

He has exposed Americans abroad and Americans in every U.S. town and city to a greater danger of attack by terrorists because of his arrogance, willfulness, and bungling at stirring up hornet's nests that pose no threat whatsoever to us. And by then insulting the religion and culture and tradition of people in other countries. And by pursuing policies that have resulted in the deaths of thousands of innocent men, women and children, all of it done in our name. . . .

> *How did we get from September 12th, 2001, . . . when we had the good will and empathy of all the world—to the horror that we all felt in witnessing the pictures of torture in Abu Ghraib?*

And the worst still lies ahead. General Joseph Hoar, [a former commander in chief of US Central Command], said "I believe we are absolutely on the brink of failure. We are looking into the abyss."

When a senior, respected military leader like Joe Hoar uses the word "abyss", then the rest of us damn well better listen. Here is what he means: more American soldiers dying, Iraq slipping into worse chaos and violence, no end in sight, with our influence and moral authority seriously damaged.

Retired Marine Corps General Anthony Zinni, who headed Central Command before becoming President Bush's personal emissary to the Middle East, said recently that our nation's current course is "headed over Niagara Falls." . . .

In his upcoming book, Zinni blames the current catastrophe on the Bush team's incompetence early on. "In the lead-up to the Iraq war, and its later conduct," he writes, "I saw at a minimum, true dereliction, negligence and irresponsibility, at worst, lying, incompetence and corruption."

Zinni's book will join a growing library of volumes by former advisors to Bush—including his principal advisor on terrorism, Richard Clarke; his principal economic policy advisor, former Treasury Secretary Paul O'Neill, former Ambassador Joe Wilson, who was honored by Bush's father [former president George H.W. Bush] for his service in Iraq, and his former Domestic Adviser on faith-based organizations, John DiIulio, who said, "There is no precedent in any modern White House for what is going on in this one: a complete lack of a policy apparatus. What you've got is everything, and I mean everything, run by the political arm. . . ."

Army Chief of Staff General Eric Shinseki told Congress in February [2004] that the occupation could require "several hundred thousand troops." But because [Secretary of Defense Donald] Rumsfeld and Bush did not want to hear disagreement with their view that Iraq could be invaded at a much lower cost, Shinseki was hushed and then forced out.

The Bush Administration Is Responsible for Prisoner Abuse

And as a direct result of this incompetent plan and inadequate troop strength, young soldiers were put in an untenable position. For example, young reservists assigned to the Iraqi prisons were called up without training or adequate supervision, and were instructed by their superiors to "break down" prisoners in order to prepare them for interrogation.

To make matters worse, they ware placed in a confusing situation where the chain of command was criss-crossed between intelligence gathering and prison administration, and further confused by an unprecedented mixing of military and civilian contractor authority.

The soldiers who are accused of committing these atrocities are, of course, responsible for their own actions and if found guilty, must be severely and appropriately punished. But they are not the ones primarily responsible for the disgrace that has been brought upon the United States of America.

Private Lynndie England [who was photographed abusing Iraqi prisoners] did not make the decision that the United States would not observe the Geneva Convention. Specialist Charles Graner was not the one who approved a policy of establishing an American Gulag of dark rooms with naked prisoners to be "stressed" and even—we must use the word—tortured—to force them to say things that legal procedures might not induce them to say.

These policies were designed and insisted upon by the Bush White House. Indeed, the President's own legal counsel advised him specifically on the subject. His secretary of defense and his assistants pushed these cruel departures from historic American standards over the objections of the uniformed military, just as the Judge Advocates General within the Defense Department were so upset and opposed that they took the unprecedented step of seeking help from a private lawyer in this city who specializes in human rights and said to him, "There is a calculated effort to create an atmosphere of legal ambiguity where the mistreatment of prisoners is concerned."

Indeed, the secrecy of the program indicates an understanding that the regular military culture and mores would not support these activities and neither would the American public or the world community. Another implicit acknowledgement of violations of accepted standards of behavior is the process of farming out prisoners to countries less averse to torture and giving assignments to private contractors.

> *When a senior, respected military leader like Joe Hoar uses the word 'abyss', then the rest of us damn well better listen.*

President Bush set the tone for our altitude for suspects in his [2003] State of the Union address. He noted that more than 3,000 "suspected terrorists" had been arrested in many countries and then he added, "and many others have met a different fate. Let's put it this way: they are no longer a problem to the United States and our allies."

George Bush promised to change the tone in Washington. And indeed he did. As many as 37 prisoners may have been murdered while in captivity, though the numbers are difficult to rely upon because in many cases involving violent death, there were no autopsies.

"Dishonor and Disgrace"

How dare they blame their misdeeds on enlisted personnel from a Reserve unit in upstate New York. President Bush owes more than one apology. On the list of those he let down are the young soldiers who are themselves apparently culpable, but who were clearly put into a moral cesspool. The perpetrators as well as the victims were both placed in their relationship to one another by the policies of George W. Bush.

How dare the incompetent and willful members of this

Bush/Cheney Administration humiliate our nation and our people in the eyes of the world and in the conscience of our own people. How dare they subject us to such dishonor and disgrace. How dare they drag the good name of the United States of America through the mud of [former Iraqi dictator] Saddam Hussein's torture prison. . . .

> *The soldiers who are accused of committing these atrocities are . . . not the ones primarily responsible for the disgrace that has been brought upon the United States of America.*

Make no mistake, the damage done at Abu Ghraib is not only to America's reputation and America's strategic interests, but also to America's spirit. It is also crucial for our nation to recognize—and to recognize quickly—that the damage our nation has suffered in the world is far, far more serious than President Bush's belated and tepid response would lead people to believe. Remember how shocked each of us, individually, was when we first saw those hideous images. The natural tendency was to first recoil from the images, and then to assume that they represented a strange and rare aberration that resulted from a few twisted minds or, as the Pentagon assured us, "a few bad apples."

But as today's shocking news reaffirms yet again, this was not rare. It was not an aberration. Today's *New York Times* reports that an Army survey of prisoner deaths and mistreatment in Iraq and Afghanisatan "show a widespread pattern of abuse involving more military units than previously known."

Nor did these abuses spring from a few twisted minds at the lowest ranks of our military enlisted personnel. No, it came from twisted values and atrocious policies at the highest levels of our government. This was done in our name, by our leaders.

A Blow to America's Moral Authority

These horrors were the predictable consequence of policy choices that flowed directly from this administration's contempt for the rule of law. And the dominance they have been seeking is truly not simply unworthy of America—it is also an illusory goal in its own right.

Our world is unconquerable because the human spirit is unconquerable, and any national strategy based on pursuing the goal of domination is doomed to fail because it generates its own opposition, and in the process, creates enemies for the would-be dominator.

A policy based on domination of the rest of the world not only creates enemies for the United States and creates recruits for [the terrorist group Al Qaeda] it also undermines the international cooperation that is essential to defeating the efforts of terrorists who wish [to] harm and intimidate Americans.

Unilateralism, as we have painfully seen in Iraq, is its own reward. Going it alone may satisfy a political instinct but it is dangerous to our military, even without their Commander in Chief taunting terrorists to "bring it on."

Our troops are stretched thin and exhausted not only because Secretary Rumsfeld contemptuously dismissed the advice of military leaders on the size of the needed force—but also because President Bush's contempt for traditional allies and international opinion left us without a real coalition to share the military and financial burden of the war and the occupation. Our future is dependent upon increasing cooperation and interdependence in a world tied ever more closely together by technologies of communications and travel. The emergence of a truly global civilization has been accompanied by the recognition of truly global challenges that require global responses that, as often as not, can only be led by the United States—and only if the United States restores and maintains its moral authority to lead.

Make no mistake, it is precisely our moral authority that is our greatest source of strength, and it is precisely our moral authority that has been recklessly put at risk by the cheap calculations and mean compromises of conscience wagered with history by this willful president. . . .

President Bush Has Shamed America

We have seen the pictures. We have learned the news. We cannot unlearn it; it is part of us. The important question now is, what will we do now about torture. Stop it? Yes, of course. But that means demanding all of the facts, not covering them up, as some now charge the administration is now doing. One of the whistleblowers at Abu Ghraib, Sergeant Samuel Provance, told ABC News that he was being intimidated and punished for telling the truth. "There is definitely a coverup," Provance said. "I feel like I am being punished for being honest."

The abhorrent acts in the prison were a direct consequence of the culture of impunity encouraged, authorized and instituted by Bush and Rumsfeld in their statements that the Geneva Conventions did not apply.[3] The apparent war crimes that took place were the logical, inevitable outcome of policies and statements from the administration.

> *How dare they drag the good name of the United States of America through the mud of Saddam Hussein's torture prison.*

To me, as glaring as the evidence of this in the pictures themselves was the revelation that it was established practice for prisoners to be moved around during ICRC [the International Committee of the Red Cross] visits so that they would not be available for visits. That, no one can claim, was the act of individuals. That was policy set from above with the direct intention to violate U.S. values it was to be upholding. It was the kind of policy we see—and criticize—in places like China and Cuba.

Moreover, the administration has also set up the men and women of our own armed forces for payback the next time they are held as prisoners. And for that, this administration should pay a very high price. One of the most tragic consequences of these official crimes is that it will be very hard for any of us as Americans—at least for a very long time—to effectively stand up for human rights elsewhere and criticize other governments, when our policies have resulted in our soldiers behaving so monstrously. This administration has shamed America and deeply damaged the cause of freedom and human rights everywhere, thus undermining the core message of America to the world.

President Bush offered a brief and half-hearted apology to the Arab world—but he should apologize to the American people for abandoning the Geneva Conventions. He also owes

3. The terrorists that have been captured in the war on terror do not fight on behalf of a nation, and do not follow warfare rules of the Geneva Convention such as wearing a clearly marked uniform. The Bush Administration has therefore argued that the sections of the Geneva Convention that require prisoners of war to be treated ethically do not apply to these prisoners.

an apology to the U.S. Army for cavalierly sending them into harm's way while ignoring the best advice of their commanders. Perhaps most importantly of all, he should apologize to all those men and women throughout our world who have held the ideal of the United States of America as a shining goal, to inspire their hopeful efforts to bring about justice under a rule of law in their own lands. Of course, the problem with all these legitimate requests is that a sincere apology requires an admission of error, a willingness to accept responsibility and to hold people accountable. And President Bush is not only unwilling to acknowledge error. He has thus far been unwilling to hold anyone in his administration accountable for the worst strategic and military miscalculations and mistakes in the history of the United States of America.

> *The damage done at Abu Ghraib is not only to America's reputation and America's strategic interests, but also to America's spirit.*

He is willing only to apologize for the alleged erratic behavior of a few low-ranking enlisted people, who he is scapegoating for his policy fiasco.

Bearing Responsibility

In December of 2000, even though I strongly disagreed with the decision by the U.S. Supreme Court to order a halt to the counting of legally cast ballots,[4] I saw it as my duty to reaffirm my own strong belief that we are a nation of laws and not only accept the decision, but do what I could to prevent efforts to delegitimize George Bush as he took the oath of office as president.

I did not at that moment imagine that Bush would, in the presidency that ensued, demonstrate utter contempt for the rule of law and work at every turn to frustrate accountability. . . .

4. Due to a breakdown in voting tabulation during the presidential election of 2000, the ballots of Florida voters had to be counted by hand. The Supreme Court eventually ended this time-consuming process so the nation could decisively name a leader. The decision was fraught with controversy, as many people argued that had the votes continued to be counted, Al Gore would have been named president instead of George W. Bush.

So today, I want to speak on behalf of those Americans who feel that President Bush has betrayed our nation's trust, those who are horrified at what has been done in our name, and all those who want the rest of the world to know that we Americans see the abuses that occurred in the prisons of Iraq, Afghanistan, Guantanamo [Bay, Cuba] and secret locations as yet undisclosed as completely out of keeping with the character and basic nature of the American people and at odds with the principles on which America stands.

I believe we have a duty to hold President Bush accountable—and I believe we will. As [former president Abraham] Lincoln said at our time of greatest trial [the Civil War], "We—even we here—hold the power, and bear the responsibility."

8

America Sends Its Prisoners of War to Other Countries to Be Tortured

Dana Priest and Barton Gellman

Dana Priest and Barton Gellman are staff writers for the Washington Post.

Since the war on terror began, the United States has been sending terror suspects to foreign countries to be interrogated. Most of these countries are thought to use torture to extract information from suspects. Although the United States publicly denies that it allows other countries to torture terror suspects, certain administration officials have confirmed that the United States encourages foreign intelligence services to extract information from terrorists by whatever means possible.

D eep inside the forbidden zone at the U.S.-occupied Bagram air base in Afghanistan, around the corner from the detention center and beyond the segregated clandestine military units, sits a cluster of metal shipping containers protected by a triple layer of concertina wire. The containers hold the most valuable prizes in the war on terrorism—captured al Qaeda operatives and Taliban commanders.[1]

1. Taliban commanders sheltered members of the terrorist group al Qaeda, and were deposed in October 2001 by a U.S.-led coalition.

Those who refuse to cooperate inside this secret CIA interrogation center are sometimes kept standing or kneeling for hours, in black hoods or spray-painted goggles, according to intelligence specialists familiar with CIA interrogation methods. At times they are held in awkward, painful positions and deprived of sleep with a 24-hour bombardment of lights—subject to what are known as "stress and duress" techniques.

Those who cooperate are rewarded with creature comforts, interrogators whose methods include feigned friendship, respect, cultural sensitivity and, in some cases, money. Some who do not cooperate are turned over—"rendered," in official parlance—to foreign intelligence services whose practice of torture has been documented by the U.S. government and human rights organizations.

A Brass-Knuckled Quest for Information

In the multifaceted global war on terrorism waged by the Bush administration, one of the most opaque—yet vital—fronts is the detention and interrogation of terrorism suspects. U.S. officials have said little publicly about the captives' names, numbers or whereabouts, and virtually nothing about interrogation methods. But interviews with several former intelligence officials and 10 current U.S. national security officials—including several people who witnessed the handling of prisoners—provide insight into how the U.S. government is prosecuting this part of the war.

> *In the multifaceted global war on terrorism waged by the Bush administration, one of the most opaque—yet vital—fronts is the detention and interrogation of terrorism suspects.*

The picture that emerges is of a brass-knuckled quest for information, often in concert with allies of dubious human rights reputation, in which the traditional lines between right and wrong, legal and inhumane, are evolving and blurred.

While the U.S. government publicly denounces the use of torture, each of the current national security officials interviewed for this article defended the use of violence against captives as just and necessary. They expressed confidence that the American public would back their view. The CIA, which has primary responsibility for interrogations, declined to comment.

> **//** *These 'extraordinary renditions' are done without resort to legal process and usually involve countries with security services known for using brutal means.* **//**

"If you don't violate someone's human rights some of the time, you probably aren't doing your job," said one official who has supervised the capture and transfer of accused terrorists. "I don't think we want to be promoting a view of zero tolerance on this. That was the whole problem for a long time with the CIA."

The off-limits patch of ground at Bagram is one of a number of secret detention centers overseas where U.S. due process[2] does not apply, according to several U.S. and European national security officials, where the CIA undertakes or manages the interrogation of suspected terrorists. Another is Diego Garcia, a somewhat horseshoe-shaped island in the Indian Ocean that the United States leases from Britain.

U.S. officials oversee most of the interrogations, especially those of the most senior captives. In some cases, highly trained CIA officers question captives through interpreters. In others, the intelligence agency undertakes a "false flag" operation using fake decor and disguises meant to deceive a captive into thinking he is imprisoned in a country with a reputation for brutality, when, in reality, he is still in CIA hands. Sometimes, female officers conduct interrogations, a psychologically jarring experience for men reared in a conservative Muslim culture where women are never in control.

"We Send Them to Other Countries"

In other cases, usually involving lower-level captives, the CIA hands them to foreign intelligence services—notably those of Jordan, Egypt and Morocco—with a list of questions the agency

2. a term referring to fundamental legal rights, such as the right to be heard, the right to a fair trial, and the right to an impartial jury

wants answered. These "extraordinary renditions" are done without resort to legal process and usually involve countries with security services known for using brutal means.

According to U.S. officials, nearly 3,000 suspected al Qaeda members and their supporters have been detained worldwide since [the terrorist attacks of] Sept. 11, 2001. About 625 are at the U.S. military's confinement facility at Guantanamo Bay, Cuba. Some officials estimated that fewer than 100 captives have been rendered to third countries. Thousands have been arrested and held with U.S. assistance in countries known for brutal treatment of prisoners, the officials said.

At a Sept. 26 [2002] joint hearing of the House and Senate intelligence committees, Cofer Black, then head of the CIA Counterterrorist Center, spoke cryptically about the agency's new forms of "operational flexibility" in dealing with suspected terrorists. "This is a very highly classified area, but I have to say that all you need to know: There was a before 9/11, and there was an after 9/11," Black said. "After 9/11 the gloves come off."

> *There was a before 9/11, and there was an after 9/11. . . . After 9/11 the gloves come off.*

According to one official who has been directly involved in rendering captives into foreign hands, the understanding is, "We don't kick the [expletive] out of them. We send them to other countries so *they* can kick the [expletive] out of them." Some countries are known to use mind-altering drugs such as sodium pentathol, said other officials involved in the process.

Abu Zubaida, who is believed to be the most important al Qaeda member in detention, was shot in the groin during his apprehension in Pakistan in March. National security officials suggested that Zubaida's painkillers were used selectively in the beginning of his captivity. He is now said to be cooperating, and his information has led to the apprehension of other al Qaeda members. . . .

U.S. officials who defend the renditions say the prisoners are sent to these third countries not because of their coercive questioning techniques, but because of their cultural affinity with the captives. Besides being illegal, they said, torture produces unreliable information from people who are desperate to stop the pain. They look to foreign allies more because their intelligence services can develop a culture of intimacy that Americans cannot. They may use interrogators who speak the captive's Arabic dialect and often use the prospects of shame and the reputation of the captive's family to goad the captive into talking.

Interrogations Yield Valuable Information

In a speech on Dec. 11 [2002], CIA director George J. Tenet said that interrogations overseas have yielded significant returns recently. He calculated that worldwide efforts to capture or kill terrorists had eliminated about one-third of the al Qaeda leadership. "Almost half of our successes against senior al Qaeda members has come in recent months," he said.

Many of these successes have come as a result of information gained during interrogations. The capture of al Qaeda leaders Ramzi Binalshibh in Pakistan, Omar al-Faruq in Indonesia, Abd al-Rahim al-Nashiri in Kuwait and Muhammad al Darbi in Yemen were all partly the result of information gained during interrogations, according to U.S. intelligence and national security officials. All four remain under CIA control.

Time, rather than technique, has produced the most helpful information, several national security and intelligence officials said. Using its global computer database, the CIA is able to quickly check leads from captives in one country with information divulged by captives in another.

"We know so much more about them now than we did a year ago—the personalities, how the networks are established, what they think are important targets, how they think we will react," said retired Army general Wayne Downing, the Bush administration's deputy national security adviser for combating terrorism until he resigned in June [2002].

"The interrogations of Abu Zubaida drove me nuts at times," Downing said. "He and some of the others are very clever guys. At times I felt we were in a classic counter-interrogation class: They were telling us what they think we already knew. Then, what they thought we wanted to know. As they did that, they fabricated and weaved in threads that went nowhere. But, even with these ploys, we still get valuable information and they are off the street, unable to plot and coordinate future attacks."

In contrast to the detention center at Guantanamo Bay, where military lawyers, news reporters and the Red Cross [a humanitarian group] received occasional access to monitor prisoner conditions and treatment, the CIA's overseas interrogation facilities are off-limits to outsiders, and often even to other government agencies. In addition to Bagram and Diego Garcia, the CIA has other secret detention centers overseas, and often uses the facilities of foreign intelligence services.

> *The most frequently alleged methods of torture include sleep deprivation, beatings on the soles of the feet, prolonged suspension with ropes in contorted positions and extended solitary confinement.*

Free from the scrutiny of military lawyers steeped in the international laws of war, the CIA and its intelligence service allies have the leeway to exert physically and psychologically aggressive techniques, said national security officials and U.S. and European intelligence officers.

Although no direct evidence of mistreatment of prisoners in U.S. custody has come to light [as of December 2002], the prisoners are denied access to lawyers or organizations, such as the Red Cross, that could independently assess their treatment. Even their names are secret. . . .

Piercing a Prisoner's Resistance

Al Qaeda suspects are seldom taken without force, and some suspects have been wounded during their capture. After apprehending suspects, U.S. take-down teams—a mix of military special forces, FBI agents, CIA case officers and local allies—aim to disorient and intimidate them on the way to detention facilities.

According to Americans with direct knowledge and others who have witnessed the treatment, captives are often "softened up" by MPs [military police] and U.S. Army Special Forces troops who beat them up and confine them in tiny rooms. The alleged terrorists are commonly blindfolded and thrown into walls, bound in painful positions, subjected to loud noises and deprived of sleep. The tone of intimidation and fear is the beginning, they said, of a process of piercing a prisoner's resistance.

The take-down teams often "package" prisoners for transport, fitting them with hoods and gags, and binding them to stretchers with duct tape.

Bush administration appointees and career national security officials acknowledged that, as one of them put it, "our guys may kick them around a little bit in the adrenaline of the immediate aftermath." Another said U.S. personnel are scrupulous in providing medical care to captives, adding in a deadpan voice, that "pain control [in wounded patients] is a very subjective thing."

"We're Not Aware of Any Torture"

The CIA's participation in the interrogation of rendered terrorist suspects varies from country to country.

"In some cases [involving interrogations in Saudi Arabia], we're able to observe through one-way mirrors the live investigations," said a senior U.S. official involved in Middle East security issues. "In others, we usually get summaries. We will feed questions to their investigators. They're still very much in control."

The official added: "We're not aware of any torture or even physical abuse." Tenet acknowledged the Saudis' role in his Dec. 11 [2002] speech. "The Saudis are [providing] increasingly important support to our counterterrorism efforts—from making arrests to sharing debriefing results," he said.

But Saudi Arabia is also said to withhold information that might lead the U.S. government to conclusions or policies that the Saudi royal family fears. U.S. teams, for that reason, have sometimes sent Saudi nationals to Egypt instead.

> *In at least one case, U.S. operatives led the capture and transfer of an al Qaeda suspect to Syria, which for years has been near the top of U.S. lists of human rights violators.*

Jordan is a favored country for renditions, several U.S. officials said. The Jordanians are considered "highly professional" interrogators, which some officials said meant that they do not use torture. But the State Department's 2001 human rights report criticized Jordan and its General Intelligence Directorate for arbitrary and unlawful detentions and abuse.

"The most frequently alleged methods of torture include sleep deprivation, beatings on the soles of the feet, prolonged suspension with ropes in contorted positions and extended solitary confinement," the 2001 report noted. Jordan also is known to use prisoners' family members to induce suspects to talk.

Another significant destination for rendered suspects is Morocco, whose general intelligence service has sharply stepped up cooperation with the United States. Morocco has a documented history of torture, as well as longstanding ties to the CIA.

> *If we're not there in the room, who is to say?*

The State Department's human rights report says Moroccan law "prohibits torture, and the government claims that the use of torture has been discontinued; however, some members of the security forces still tortured or otherwise abused detainees."

In at least one case, U.S. operatives led the capture and transfer of an al Qaeda suspect to Syria, which for years has been near the top of U.S. lists of human rights violators and sponsors of terrorism. The German government strongly protested the move. The suspect, Mohammed Haydar Zammar, holds joint German and Syrian citizenship. It could not be learned how much of Zammar's interrogation record Syria has provided the CIA.

Using the Fruits of Torture

The Bush administration maintains a legal distance from any mistreatment that occurs overseas, officials said, by denying that torture is the intended result of its rendition policy. American teams, officials said, do no more than assist in the transfer of suspects who are wanted on criminal charges by friendly countries. But five officials acknowledged, as one of them put it, "that sometimes a friendly country can be invited to 'want' someone we grab." Then, other officials said, the foreign government will charge him with a crime of some sort.

One official who has had direct involvement in renditions said he knew they were likely to be tortured. "I . . . do it with my eyes open," he said.

According to present and former officials with firsthand knowledge, the CIA's authoritative Directorate of Operations instructions, drafted in cooperation with the general counsel, tells case officers in the field that they may not engage in, provide advice about or encourage the use of torture by cooperating intelligence services from other countries. . . .

Said Fred Hitz, former CIA inspector general, "we don't do torture, and we can't countenance torture in terms of we can't know of it." But if a country offers information gleaned from interrogations, "we can use the fruits of it."

Bush administration officials said the CIA, in practice, is using a narrow definition of what counts as "knowing" that a suspect has been tortured. "If we're not there in the room, who is to say?" said one official conversant with recent reports of renditions.

The Clinton administration pioneered the use of extraordinary rendition after the bombings of U.S. embassies in Kenya and Tanzania in 1998. But it also pressed allied intelligence services to respect lawful boundaries in interrogations.

After years of fruitless talks in Egypt, President Bill Clinton cut off funding and cooperation with the directorate of Egypt's general intelligence service, whose torture of suspects has been a perennial theme in State Department human rights reports.

"You can be sure," one Bush administration official said, "that we are not spending a lot of time on that now."

9

The Torture of Iraqi Prisoners Was an Aberration

Donald Rumsfeld

Donald Rumsfeld is secretary of defense for the Bush administration.

Editor's Note: The following viewpoint was originally given as testimony before the Senate and House Armed Services committees on May 7, 2004.

A few corrupt soldiers abused inmates at Abu Ghraib prison in Iraq in 2004. Their behavior sharply deviated from the U.S. Army's standards of soldier conduct. The abuses were the crimes of the soldiers alone—they did not result from a lack of training or from a climate of abuse present in the army. Indeed, the military has taken responsibility for the Abu Ghraib incident by being the first to expose the abuses and thoroughly investigating its own personnel. These swift and decisive actions have led to important changes that will prevent future abuse of prisoners in the army's custody. Although the abuses are regrettable, America has admirably handled the crisis in a democratic fashion, which proves its commitment to human rights and freedom.

In recent days, there has been a good deal of discussion about who bears responsibility for the terrible activities that took place at Abu Ghraib [prison, where Iraqi prisoners were abused by U.S. soldiers]. These events occurred on my watch. As Sec-

Donald Rumsfeld, testimony before the Senate and House Armed Services committees, Washington, DC, May 7, 2004.

retary of Defense, I am accountable for them. I take full responsibility. It is my obligation to evaluate what happened, to make sure those who have committed wrongdoing are brought to justice, and to make changes as needed to see that it doesn't happen again.

Apologies Are Due

I feel terrible about what happened to these Iraqi detainees. They are human beings. They were in U.S. custody. Our country had an obligation to treat them right. We didn't do that. That was wrong.

To those Iraqis who were mistreated by members of U.S. armed forces, I offer my deepest apology. It was un-American. And it was inconsistent with the values of our nation.

Further, I deeply regret the damage that has been done:
- First, to the reputation of the honorable men and women of our armed forces who are courageously, skillfully and responsibly defending our freedom across the globe. They are truly wonderful human beings, and their families and loved ones can be enormously proud of them.
- Second, to the President, the Congress and the American people. I wish we had been able to convey to them the gravity of this before we saw it in the media;
- Third, to the Iraqi people, whose trust in our coalition has been shaken; and finally
- To the reputation of our country.

The photographic depictions of U.S. military personnel [abusing Iraqi prisoners] that the public has seen have unquestionably offended and outraged everyone in the Department of Defense [DOD].

If you could have seen the anguished expressions on the faces of those of us in the Department upon seeing the photos, you would know how we feel today.

We take this seriously. It should not have happened. Any wrongdoers need to be punished, procedures evaluated, and problems corrected.

It's important for the American people and the world to know that while these terrible acts were perpetrated by a small number of the U.S. military, they were also brought to light by the honorable and responsible action of other military personnel. There are many who did their duty professionally and we should mention that as well:

- First the soldier, Specialist Joseph Darby, who alerted the appropriate authorities that abuses of detainees were occurring. My thanks and appreciation to him for his courage and his values.
- Second, those in the military chain of command who acted promptly upon learning of those activities by initiating a series of investigations—criminal and administrative—to ensure that the abuses were stopped, that the responsible chain of command was relieved and replaced, and that the Uniform Code of Military Justice was followed.
- Third, units singled out for praise in General [Antonio] Taguba's Report [which investigated the abuse incidents] for the care they provided detainees in their custody and their intolerance of abuses by others.
- And finally, the CENTCOM [U.S. Central Command] chain of command for taking action and publicly announcing to the world that investigations of abuse were underway.

"We Want You to Know the Facts"

The American people and members of the committee deserve an accounting of what has happened and what's being done to fix it.

Gathered today are the senior military officials with responsibility in the care and treatment of detainees.

The responsibility for training falls to the U.S. Army. The responsibility for the actions and conduct of forces in Iraq falls to the combatant commander. And the ultimate responsibility for the department rests with me.

Each of us has had a strong interest in getting the facts out to the American people.

We want you to know the facts. I want you to have all the documentation and the data you require. If some material is classified, we will ensure members get an opportunity to see it privately.

Having said that, all the facts that may be of interest are not yet in hand. In addition to the Taguba Report, there are other investigations underway. We will make the results of these investigations available to you. But because all the facts are not in hand, there will be corrections and clarifications to the record as more information is learned. If we have something to add later, we'll do so. If we find something that we've said that needs to be corrected, we'll correct it.

From the other witnesses here, you will be told the sequence of events and investigations that have taken place since these activities first came to light.

What I want to do is to inform you of the measures underway to remedy some of the damage done and to improve our performance in the future.

> **❝ I feel terrible about what happened to these Iraqi detainees. ❞**

Before I do that, let me make one further note: As members of this Committee are aware, each of us at this table is either in the chain of command or has senior responsibilities in the Department. This means that anything we say publicly could have an impact on legal proceedings against those accused of wrongdoing in this matter. Our responsibility at this hearing, and in our public comments, is to conduct ourselves consistent with that well known fact. So please understand that if some of our responses are measured, it is to ensure that pending cases are not jeopardized by seeming to exert "command influence" and that the rights of any accused are protected.

Now let me tell you the measures we are taking to deal with this issue.

The Crimes Are Being Investigated

When this incident came to light and was reported within the Chain of Command, we took several immediate actions. These will be discussed in detail by others here today, but let me highlight them:

- General [Ricardo] Sanchez launched a criminal investigation immediately.
- He then asked for an administrative review of procedures at the Abu Ghraib facility. That is the so-called Taguba Report.

These two investigations have resulted thus far in criminal or administrative actions against at least 12 individuals, including the relief of the prison chain of command and criminal referrals of several soldiers directly involved in abuse:

- The Army also launched an Inspector General Review of detainee operations throughout Afghanistan and Iraq. That review continues.
- The Army has initiated an investigation of Reserve training with respect to military intelligence and police functions.
- General Sanchez also asked for an Army Intelligence review of the circumstances discussed in General Taguba's report and that is ongoing.
- And, I also asked the Navy Inspector General to review procedures at Guantanamo [Bay, Cuba] and the Charleston Naval Brig [where other detainees from the war on terror are being held].

As these investigations mature, we will endeavor to keep you informed. But there is more to be done.

Changes Will Be Made

First, to ensure we have a handle on the scope of this catastrophe, I will be announcing today the appointment of several senior former officials who are being asked to examine the pace, breadth, and thoroughness of the existing investigations, and to determine whether additional investigations need to be initiated. They are being asked to report their findings within 45 days of taking up their duties. I am confident these distinguished individuals will provide a full and fair assessment of what has been done thus far—and recommend whether further steps may be necessary.

> *It's important for the American people and the world to know that . . . these terrible acts were perpetrated by a small number of the U.S. military.*

I will encourage them to meet with members of Congress to keep them apprised of their progress. I look forward to their suggestions and recommendations.

Second, we need to review our habits and procedures. One of the things we've tried to do since [the terrorist attacks of] September 11th [2001] to get the Department to adjust its habits and procedures at a time of war, and in the information age. For the past three years, we have looked for areas where adjustments were needed, and regrettably, we have now found another one.

> *I know that we did not fully brief you on this subject along the way and we should have done so.*

Let me be clear. I failed to identify the catastrophic damage that the allegations of abuse could do to our operations in the theater [that is, the battlefield], to the safety of our troops in the field, the cause to which we are committed. When these allegations first surfaced, I failed to recognize how important it was to elevate a matter of such gravity to the highest levels, including leaders in Congress. Nor did we anticipate that a classified investigation report that had not yet been delivered to the senior levels of the Department would be given to the media. That was my failing.

In the future, we will take whatever steps are necessary to elevate to the appropriate levels charges of this magnitude.

Third, I am seeking a way to provide appropriate compensation to those detainees who suffered grievous and brutal abuse and cruelty at the hands of a few members of the U.S. military. It is the right thing to do. I'm told we have the ability to do so. And so we will—one way or another.

"I Know That We Did Not Fully Brief You"

One of the great strengths of our nation is its ability to recognize failures, deal with them, and to strive to make things better. Indeed, the openness with which these problems are being dealt is one of the strengths of our free society. Democracies are imperfect, because they are made up of human beings who are, by our nature, imperfect. Of course, we wish that every person in our government and our Armed Forces would conduct themselves in accordance with the highest standards of ethics. But the reality is some do not.

One mistake we have made during our initial investigation into these charges, for example, was failing to sufficiently call to your attention the information made public in the CENT-COM press release regarding the investigations they had initiated back in January [2004]. We also failed to sufficiently call your attention and brief you on the preliminary findings of the criminal investigation announced on March 20 [2004] by General [Mark] Kimmitt. I am advised the Army has had periodic meetings to inform Congressional staffs.

There are indications that the information provided was penetrating at some level, however. On January 20th [2004], for example, CNN reported that a CID [Criminal Investigation Division] investigation was being conducted into allegations of detainee abuse at Abu Ghraib, and mentioned the possible existence of photographs taken of detainees.

Nonetheless, I know that we did not fully brief you on this subject along the way and we should have done so.

I wish we would have known more sooner and been able to tell you more sooner. But we didn't. For that, I apologize.

We need to discuss a better way to keep you informed about matters of such gravity in the future.

> *The standard by which our country and our government should be judged is not by whether abuses take place, but rather how our nation deals with them.*

The fact that abuses take place—in the military, in law enforcement, and in our society—is not surprising. But the standard by which our country and our government should be judged is not by whether abuses take place, but rather how our nation deals with them. We are dealing with them forthrightly. These incidents are being investigated and any found to have committed crimes or misconduct will receive the appropriate justice. Most of the time, at least, the system works.

None of this is meant to diminish the gravity of the recent situation at Abu Ghraib. To the contrary, that is precisely why these abuses are so damaging—because they can be used by the enemies of our country to undermine our mission and spread the false impression that such conduct is the rule and not the exception—when, in fact, the opposite is true.

Which is why it is so important that we investigate them

publicly and openly, and hold people accountable in similar fashion. And that is exactly what we are doing.

The Abuses Were the Crimes of the Soldiers

When we first were told about these activities and saw those photographs, I and everyone at this table was as shocked and stunned as you were.

In the period since, a number of questions have been raised—here in the Congress, in the media, and by the public. Let me respond to some of them.

Some have asked: Why weren't those charged with guarding prisoners properly trained?

If one looks at the behavior depicted in those photos, it is fair to ask: what kind of training could one possibly provide that would stop people from doing that? Either you learn that in life, or you don't. And if someone doesn't know that doing what is shown in those photos is wrong, cruel, brutal, indecent, and against American values, I am at a loss as to what kind of training could be provided to teach them.

The fact is, the vast majority of the people in the United States Armed Forces are decent, honorable individuals who know right from wrong, and conduct themselves in a manner that is in keeping with the spirit and values of our country. And there is only a very small minority who do not.

> *If one looks at the behavior depicted in those photos, it is fair to ask: what kind of training could one possibly provide that would stop people from doing that?*

Some have asked: Hasn't a climate allowing for abuses to occur been created because of a decision to "disregard" the Geneva Convention?[1]

No. Indeed, the U.S. Government recognized that the Geneva Conventions apply in Iraq, and the armed forces are obliged to follow them. DOD personnel are trained in the law

1. The 1949 Geneva Convention is an internationally recognized document that protects the rights of prisoners of war.

of war, including the Geneva Conventions. Doctrine requires that they follow those rules and report, investigate, and take corrective action to remedy violations.

We did conclude that our war against [the terrorist group] al-Qaeda is not governed precisely by the Conventions, but nevertheless announced that detained individuals would be treated consistent with the principles of the Geneva Conventions.

America Values Human Life

Some have asked: Can we repair the damage done to our credibility in the region?

I hope so and I believe so. We have to trust that in the course of events the truth will eventually come out. And the truth is that the United States is a liberator, not a conqueror. Our people are devoted to freedom and democracy, not enslavement or oppression.

> **❝** *The vast majority of the people in the United States Armed Forces are decent, honorable individuals who know right from wrong.* **❞**

Every day, these men and women risk their lives to protect the Iraqi people and help them build a more hopeful future. They have liberated 25 million people; dismantled two terrorist regimes; and battled an enemy that shows no compassion or respect for innocent human life.

These men and women, and the families who love and support them, deserves better than to have their sacrifices on behalf of our country sullied by the despicable actions of a few. To that vast majority of our soldiers abroad, I extend my support and my appreciation for their truly outstanding service. . . .

Within the constraints imposed on those of us in the chain of command, I want to say a few additional words.

First, beyond abuse of prisoners, we have seen photos that depict incidents of physical violence towards prisoners—acts that may be described as blatantly sadistic, cruel, and inhuman.

Second, the individuals who took the photos took many more.

The ramifications of these two facts are far reaching.

Congress and the American people and the rest of the world need to know this.

In addition, the photos give these incidents a vividness—indeed a horror—in the eyes of the world.

> *The truth is that the United States is a liberator, not a conqueror.*

Mr. Chairman, that is why this hearing today is important. And why the actions we take in the days and weeks ahead are so important.

Because however terrible the setback, this is also an occasion to demonstrate to the world the difference between those who believe in democracy and human rights and those who believe in rule by the terrorist code.

We value human life; we believe in their right to individual freedom and the rule of law.

For those beliefs we send the men and women in the armed forces abroad—to protect that right for our own people and to give millions of others who aren't Americans the hope of a future of freedom.

Dealing with Wrongdoing Is Part of Democracy

Part of that mission—part of what we believe in—is making sure that when wrongdoing or scandal occur that they are not covered up, but exposed, investigated, publicly disclosed—and the guilty brought to justice.

Mr. Chairman, I know you join me today in saying to the world: Judge us by our actions. Watch how Americans, watch how a democracy deals with wrongdoing and scandal and the pain of acknowledging and correcting our own mistakes and weaknesses.

And then after they have seen America in action—then ask those who preach resentment and hatred of America if our behavior doesn't give the lie to the falsehood and slander they speak about our people and way of life. Ask them if the resolve of Americans in crisis and difficulty—and, yes, the heartache of acknowledging the evil in our midst—doesn't have meaning far beyond their code of hatred.

Above all, ask them if the willingness of Americans to acknowledge their own failures before humanity doesn't light the world as surely as the great ideas and beliefs that first made this nation a beacon of hope and liberty to all who strive to be free.

We know what the terrorists will do. We know they will try to exploit all that is bad to obscure all that is good. That is the nature of evil. And that is the nature of those who think they can kill innocent men, women and children to gratify their own cruel will to power.

We say to the enemies of humanity and freedom:

Do your worst.

Because we will strive to do our best.

10

Leadership Failures Facilitated the Abuses at Abu Ghraib Prison in Iraq

James R. Schlesinger et al.

The Schlesinger report was chaired by James R. Schlesinger, and included panel members Harold Brown, Tillie K. Fowler, and Charles A. Horner. The executive director of the panel was James A. Blackwell Jr.

The abuses that occurred at Abu Ghraib prison in Iraq were the result of a breakdown of leadership and mis-applied interrogation tactics. Such abuses could have been prevented with clearer interrogation guidelines, better leadership, and more training for inexperienced soldiers. Instances of abuse have been found to occur at U.S. military facilities in other parts of the world, in-dicating that abuse by American military personnel is more widespread than initially thought. Although the abuses were not sanctioned by any official army policy, the Department of Defense must critically reexamine its methods to ensure that abuse of prisoners in U.S. care does not happen again.

Editor's Note: After it came to light that U.S. soldiers had abused Iraqi prisoners at Abu Ghraib prison in Iraq, several investigations were launched to uncover how the abuses had occurred and who was responsible for them. The following excerpt is from the Schlesinger re-port, widely regarded as the most independent panel commissioned to investigate the abuse scandal.

James R. Schlesinger, Harold Brown, Tillie K. Fowler, Charles A. Horner, and James A. Blackwell Jr., *Final Report of the Independent Panel to Review DoD Detention Operations*, www.defenselink.mil, August 24, 2004.

The events of October through December 2003 on the night shift of Tier 1 at Abu Ghraib prison were acts of brutality and purposeless sadism.[1] We now know these abuses occurred at the hands of both military police [MP] and military intelligence [MI] personnel. The pictured abuses, unacceptable even in wartime, were not part of authorized interrogations nor were they even directed at intelligence targets. They represent deviant behavior and a failure of military leadership and discipline. However, we do know that some of the egregious abuses at Abu Ghraib which were not photographed did occur during interrogation sessions and that abuses during interrogation sessions occurred elsewhere [at other holding facilities around the world].

> *The abuses were not just the failure of some individuals to follow known standards, and they are more than the failure of a few leaders to enforce proper discipline.*

In light of what happened at Abu Ghraib, a series of comprehensive investigations has been conducted by various components of the Department of Defense [DoD]. Since the beginning of hostilities in Afghanistan [in 2001] and Iraq [in 2003], U.S. military and security operations have apprehended about 50,000 individuals. From this number, about 300 allegations of abuse in Afghanistan, Iraq or Guantanamo [Bay, Cuba, where detainees from the war on terror are held] have arisen. As of mid-August 2004, 155 investigations into the allegations have been completed, resulting in 66 substantiated cases. Approximately one-third of these cases occurred at the point of capture or tactical collection point, frequently under uncertain, dangerous and violent circumstances.

Abuses of varying severity occurred at differing locations under differing circumstances and context. They were widespread and, though inflicted on only a small percentage of

---

1. In the spring of 2004 it came to light that terrible abuses had been committed at Abu Ghraib prison in Iraq. Prisoners were tortured, abused, and humiliated by several American soldiers. Shocking photographs of the abuses were disseminated by the media.

those detained, they were serious both in number and in effect. No approved procedures called for or allowed the kinds of abuse that in fact occurred. There is no evidence of a policy of abuse promulgated by senior officials or military authorities. Still, the abuses were not just the failure of some individuals to follow known standards, and they are more than the failure of a few leaders to enforce proper discipline. There is both institutional and personal responsibility at higher levels. . . .

Abuses Could Have Been Prevented

Of the 66 already substantiated cases of abuse, eight occurred at Guantanamo, three in Afghanistan and 55 in Iraq. Only about one-third were related to interrogation, and two-thirds to other causes. There were five cases of detainee deaths as a result of abuse by U.S. personnel during interrogations. Many more died from natural causes and enemy mortar attacks. There are 23 cases of detainee deaths still under investigation; three in Afghanistan and 20 in Iraq. Twenty-eight of the abuse cases are alleged to include Special Operations Forces (SOF) and, of the 15 SOF cases that have been closed, ten were determined to be unsubstantiated and five resulted in disciplinary action. The Jacoby review of SOF detention operations found a range of abuses and causes similar in scope and magnitude to those found among conventional forces.

The aberrant behavior on the night shift in Cell Block 1 at Abu Ghraib would have been avoided with proper training, leadership and oversight. Though acts of abuse occurred at a number of locations, those in Cell Block 1 have a unique nature fostered by the predilections of the noncommissioned officers in charge. Had these noncommissioned officers behaved more like those on the day shift, these acts, which one participant described as "just for the fun of it," would not have taken place. . . .

Rough Interrogation Techniques Were Misapplied in Iraq

Interrogation policies with respect to Iraq, where the majority of the abuses occurred, were inadequate or deficient in some respects at three levels: Department of Defense, CENTCOM/ CJTF-7, and Abu Ghraib Prison. Policies to guide the demands for actionable intelligence [that is, information that can be used to catch terrorists] lagged behind battlefield needs. . . . The changes in DoD interrogation policies between December 2, 2002 and April 16, 2003 were an element contributing to uncertainties in the field as to which [interrogation] techniques were authorized.[2] Although specifically limited by the Secretary of Defense [Donald Rumsfeld] to Guantanamo, and requiring his personal approval (given in only two cases), the augmented techniques for Guantanamo [which included controversial "stress and duress" techniques of withholding food, light, sleep, and clothing to prisoners] migrated to Afghanistan and Iraq where they were neither limited nor safeguarded. . . .

> *The aberrant behavior on the night shift in Cell Block 1 at Abu Ghraib would have been avoided with proper training, leadership and oversight.*

Policies [that is, stress and duress techniques] approved for use on al Qaeda and Taliban detainees [that is, captured terrorists], who were not afforded the protection of the Geneva Conventions, now applied to detainees [in Iraq] who did fall under the Geneva Convention protections [and thus should have been legally protected from such treatment]. . . .

This clearly led to confusion on what [interrogation] practices were acceptable [at Abu Ghraib prison]. We cannot be sure how much the number and severity of abuses would have been curtailed had there been early and consistent guidance from higher levels. Nonetheless, such guidance was needed and likely would have had a limiting effect. . . .

Higher-Ups Failed to Act

[This] Panel concurs with the findings of the Taguba and Jones investigations that serious leadership problems in the 800th MP Brigade and 205th MI Brigade, to include the 320th MP

2. The authors are referring to changes to interrogation policies that were made to reflect the difference between the enemy combatants of the war on terror and traditional prisoners of war (POWs). The Bush administration has argued that because terrorists are not traditional soldiers who fight in a national army, they are not true POWs and should not receive protection under the Geneva Convention, which dictate how prisoners of war are to be treated.

Battalion Commander and the Director of the Joint Debriefing and Interrogation Center (JDIC), allowed the abuses at Abu Ghraib. The Panel endorses the disciplinary actions taken as a result of the Taguba Investigation. The Panel anticipates that the Chain of Command will take additional disciplinary action as a result of the referrals of the Jones/Fay investigation.

We believe [Lieutenant General Ricardo] Sanchez should have taken stronger action in November [2003] when he realized the extent of the leadership problems at Abu Ghraib. His attempt to mentor [the head of Abu Ghraib, Brigadier General Janis] Karpinski, though well-intended, was insufficient in a combat zone in the midst of a serious and growing insurgency. Although LTG Sanchez had more urgent tasks than dealing personally with command and resource deficiencies at Abu Ghraib, [Major General Walter] Wojdakowski and the staff should have seen that urgent demands were placed to higher headquarters for additional assets. We concur with the Jones findings that LTG Sanchez and MG Wojdakowski failed to ensure proper staff oversight of detention and interrogation operations. . . .

> *Serious leadership problems in the 800th MP Brigade and 205th MI Brigade . . . allowed the abuses at Abu Ghraib.*

Once it became clear in the summer of 2003 that there was a major insurgency growing in Iraq, with the potential for capturing a large number of enemy combatants, senior leaders should have moved to meet the need for additional military police forces. Certainly by October and November [2003] when the fighting reached a new peak, commanders and staff . . . all the way to CENTCOM to the Joint Chiefs of Staff [JCS] should have known about and reacted to the serious limitations of the battalion of the 800th Military Police Brigade at Abu Ghraib. CENTCOM and the JCS should have at least considered adding forces to the detention/interrogation operation mission. It is the judgment of this Panel that in the future, considering the sensitivity of this kind of mission, the OSD [Office of the Secretary of Defense] should assure itself that serious limitations in detention/interrogation missions do not occur.

Several options were available to Commander CENTCOM

and above, including reallocation of U.S. Army assets already in the theater [that is, the field of war], Operational Control (OPCON) of other Service Military Police units in theater, and mobilization and deployment of additional forces from the continental United States. There is no evidence that any of the responsible senior officers considered any of these options. What could and should have been done more promptly is evidenced by the fact that the detention/interrogation operation in Iraq is now directed by a Major General reporting directly to the Commander, Multi-National Forces Iraq (MNFI). Increased units of Military Police, fully manned and more appropriately equipped, are performing the mission once assigned to a single under-strength, poorly trained, inadequately equipped and weakly-led brigade.

In addition to the already cited leadership problems in the 800th MP Brigade, there were a series of tangled command relationships [at Abu Ghraib]. These ranged from an unclear military intelligence chain of command, to the Tactical Control (TACON) relationship of the 800th with CJTF-7 which the Brigade Commander apparently did not adequately understand, and the confusing and unusual assignment of MI and MP responsibilities at Abu Ghraib. The failure to react appropriately to [reports of chaos and abuse at Abu Ghraib] is indicative of the weakness of the leadership at Abu Ghraib. . . .

Abuse Must Never Happen Again

While any abuse is too much, we see signs that the Department of Defense is now on the path to dealing with the personal and professional failures and remedying the underlying causes of these abuses. We expect any potential future incidents of abuse will similarly be discovered and reported out of the same sense of personal honor and duty that characterized many of those who went out of their way to do so in most of these cases. The damage these incidents have done to U.S. policy, to the image of the U.S. among populations whose support we need in the Global War on Terror and to the morale of our armed forces, must not be repeated.

11

Detainees in Guantánamo Bay Should Have the Same Rights as Prisoners of War

Michael Byers

Michael Byers teaches international law at Duke University.

The detainees held at the U.S. facility in Guantánamo Bay, Cuba, should be granted prisoner of war (POW) status until they are deemed to be otherwise by an approved body. Although the al Qaeda and Taliban detainees are not the typical soldiers described in the 1949 Geneva Convention, which protects the rights of prisoners captured in war, they count as soldiers by the modern definition of war, and the convention's protections therefore extend to them. Only a ruling in an appropriate court can change this designation. By violating the rights of the prisoners in its custody, the United States jeopardizes its own soldiers, who may be vengefully mistreated if captured in future wars. Furthermore, the United States risks forfeiting international cooperation in the war on terror by not respecting the international laws it is party to.

Would you want your life to be in hands of U.S. Secretary of Defence Donald Rumsfeld? Hundreds of captured Taliban and al-Qaeda fighters [caught after the U.S. invasion of Af-

Michael Byers, "Ignore the Geneva Convention and Put Our Own Citizens at Risk," *The Humanist*, vol. 62, March/April 2002. Copyright © 2002 by the American Humanist Association. Reproduced by permission of the author.

ghanistan in 2001] don't have a choice. Chained, manacled, hooded, not even sedated, their beards shorn off against their will, they are being flown around the world to Guantanamo Bay, a century-old military outpost seized during the Spanish-American War and subsequently leased from Cuba by the United States. There, they are being kept in tiny chain-link outdoor cages, without mosquito repellent, where (their captors assure us) they are likely to be rained upon.

POW Status Until Proven Otherwise

Since Guantanamo Bay is technically foreign territory, the detainees have no rights under the U.S. Constitution and cannot appeal to U.S. federal courts. Any rights they might have under international law have been firmly denied. According to Rumsfeld, the detainees "will be handled not as prisoners of war, because they are not, but as unlawful combatants."

This unilateral determination of the detainees' status is highly convenient [for the Bush administration], since the 1949 Geneva Convention on the treatment of prisoners of war stipulates that POWs can only be tried by "the same courts according to the same procedure as in the case of members of the armed forces of the detaining power." The Pentagon clearly intends to prosecute at least some of the detainees in special military commissions having looser rules of evidence and a lower burden of proof than regular military or civilian courts. This will help to protect classified information but also substantially increase the likelihood of convictions. The rules of evidence and procedure for the military commissions will be issued by none other than Donald Rumsfeld.

> *The Geneva Convention . . . makes it clear that it isn't for Rumsfeld to decide whether the detainees are ordinary criminal suspects rather than POWs.*

The Geneva Convention also makes it clear that it isn't for Rumsfeld to decide whether the detainees are ordinary criminal suspects rather than POWs. Anyone detained in the course of an armed conflict is presumed to be a POW until a competent court or tribunal determines otherwise. The record shows that those who negotiated the convention were intent on making it impossible for the determination to be made by any single person.

Modern Conflicts and the Rules of War

Once in front of a court or tribunal, the Pentagon might argue that the Taliban were not the [rightful] government of Afghanistan and that their armed forces were not the armed forces of a party to the convention. The problem here is that the convention is widely regarded as an accurate statement of customary international law, unwritten rules binding on all. Even if the Taliban were not formally a party to the convention, both they and the U.S. would still have to comply.

The Pentagon might also argue that al-Qaeda members were not part of the Taliban's regular armed forces. Traditionally, irregulars could only benefit from POW status if they wore identifiable insignia, which al-Qaeda members seem not to have done. But the removal of the Taliban regime was justified on the basis that al-Qaeda and the Taliban were inextricably linked, a justification that weakens the claim that the former are irregulars [because they were fighting on behalf of government forces].

Moreover, the convention has to be interpreted in the context of modern international conflicts, which share many of the aspects of civil wars and tend not to involve professional soldiers on both sides. Since the convention is designed to protect persons, not states, the guiding principle has to be the furtherance of that protection. This principle is manifest in the presumption that every detainee is a POW until a competent court or tribunal determines otherwise.

Human Beings with Human Rights

This too is the position of the International Committee of the Red Cross, which plays a supervisory role over the convention. The Red Cross and [the human rights group] Amnesty International have both expressed concerns over the treatment of the detainees.

The authorities at Guantanamo Bay have prohibited journalists from filming the arrival of the detainees on the basis that the convention stipulates POWs "must at all times be protected against insults and public curiosity." The hypocrisy undermines the position on POW status: you can't have your cake and eat it.

> **❝** *If human rights are worth anything, they have to apply when governments are most tempted to violate them.* **❞**

Even if the detainees were not POWs, they remain human beings with human rights. Hooding, even temporarily, constitutes a violation of the 1984 convention against torture and cruel, inhuman, or degrading treatment. Apart from causing unnecessary mental anguish, it prevents a detainee from identifying anyone causing them harm. Forcefully shaving off their beards constitutes a violation of the right to human dignity under the 1966 International Covenant on Civil and Political Rights. Forcefully sedating even one detainee for nonmedical reasons violates international law. Although strict security arrangements are important in dealing with potentially dangerous individuals, none of these measures are necessary to achieving that goal. If human rights are worth anything, they have to apply when governments are most tempted to violate them.

Our Rights as Well

There are many reasons why these and other violations are unacceptable. The rights of the detainees are our rights as well. Yet international law can be modified as a result of state behaviour. If we stand by while the rights of the detainees are undermined, we, as individuals, could lose.

British and American soldiers and aid workers operate around the world in conflict zones dominated by quasi-irregular forces. The violations in Guantanamo Bay will undermine the ability of our governments to ensure adequate treatment next time our fellow citizens are captured and held. Respecting the presumption of POW status and upholding the human rights of detainees today will help to protect our people in the future.

The U.S. has occupied much of the moral high ground since [the terrorist attacks of] September 11, [2001,] and benefited enormously from so doing. Widespread sympathy for the

U.S. has made it much easier to freeze financial assets and secure the detention of suspects overseas, as well as secure intelligence sharing and military support. The sympathy has also bolstered efforts to win the hearts and minds of ordinary people in the Middle East, South Asia and elsewhere. That might just have prevented further terrorist attacks.

Ignoring even some of the rights of those detained in Guantanamo Bay squanders this intangible but invaluable asset, in return for nothing but the fleeting satisfaction of early revenge. The detainees should be accorded full treatment as POWs and, if not released in due course, tried before regular military or civilian courts—or even better, an ad hoc international tribunal. As the world watches, vengeance is ours. But so, too, are civilised standards of treatment and justice.

12

Detainees in Guantánamo Bay Should Not Have the Same Rights as Prisoners of War

Andrew Apostolou and Fredric Smoler

Andrew Apostolou is a historian at Oxford University and a writer for the Economist Intelligence Unit. *Fredric Smoler is a professor of history at Sarah Lawrence College and a contributing editor at* American Heritage *magazine.*

The al Qaeda and Taliban fighters held at U.S. detention centers have broken the codes of war set forth in the Geneva Convention of 1949, and thus are not eligible to receive protection as prisoners of war (POWs). They have actively sought to kill civilians, disguised themselves as fighters by concealing their weapons, and feigned surrender and then attacked their captors. These dubious tactics are all outside the rules of warfare to which true soldiers must adhere. Seeking POW status for these detainees is a misguided effort that not only undermines America's commitment to international law but also endangers both soldiers and civilians. The United States best respects the Geneva Convention by applying it only to those fighters who truly deserve its protection.

Andrew Apostolou and Fredric Smoler, "The Geneva Convention Is Not a Suicide Pact," *The Foundation for the Defense of Democracies*, November 6, 2002. Reproduced by permission.

In all the legal punditry and high moral posturing that has passed for analysis since Taliban[1] and al-Qaida[2] detainees arrived at Camp X-Ray in Guantánamo Bay,[3] both the purpose and origins of the 1949 Geneva Convention [which protects the rights of prisoners of war] have been too often forgotten.

The convention was not drawn up by contemporary human rights activists. Rather the Geneva Convention relative to the Treatment of Prisoners of War was adopted in 1949, after German and Japanese atrocities during the Second World War had shown up the dismal inadequacies of the Hague Convention of 1907 [an earlier document that provided rules for warfare]. The Germans had regarded entire civilian groups as enemies, to be either exterminated or forcibly and violently resettled. Both the Germans and Japanese had shot legitimate resistance members (without the barest pretence of legal process), executed commandos, and used prisoners for medical experiments. Article 4 of the 1949 Geneva Convention very deliberately extended the protections traditionally restricted to regular troops to various categories of irregulars, defining such militias with some elasticity.

> *The demand that the detainees be termed POWs is being made without any serious consideration as to whether they qualify for such protected status.*

These important protections, for soldiers, resistance fighters and civilians alike are now in serious jeopardy. The threat to the integrity of the Geneva Convention comes not from the U.S. government but from an ill-conceived and misguided campaign by human rights groups and European governments to grant prisoner-of-war (POW) status to all the Camp X-Ray detainees.

The demand that the detainees be termed POWs is being made without any serious consideration as to whether they

1. In October 2001 the U.S. invaded Afghanistan to topple the Taliban government, which had given shelter to the terrorist group al-Qaida.   2. Al-Qaida is the group responsible for several acts of terrorism against the United States, including the September 11, 2001, attacks.   3. Detainees from the war on terror are mainly held at Guantánamo Bay, Cuba, on property that the U.S. government leases from the Cuban government.

qualify for such protected status under the Geneva Convention and certainly without the slightest examination of the consequences of them receiving such a status.

Detainees Do Not Qualify as POWs

The Geneva Convention and the two additional protocols of 1977 (the U.S. has yet to ratify the latter two documents) are so broad in their protections that they include those who spontaneously seek to defend their country against aggression. The 1949 text talks of the: "Inhabitants of a non-occupied territory, who on the approach of the enemy spontaneously take up arms to resist the invading forces, without having had time to form themselves into regular armed units, provided they carry arms openly and respect the laws and customs of war" (article 4, subsection 6). Such a provision clearly does not cover the mostly Arab and Pakistani al-Qaida members now in Camp X-Ray—foreigners whom most Afghans regarded as an occupying force.

Yet the convention also deliberately places limits on who can be a POW. Acquiring this protected status depends, as noted above, on the captives having carried arms "openly" and fighting in accordance with "the laws and customs of war." The convention assumes that the captives "have laid down their arms"— that they have actually surrendered and stopped fighting.

> *Al-Qaida and Taliban fighters positively pride themselves on violating the laws of war.*

Of course, al-Qaida and Taliban fighters positively pride themselves on violating the laws of war. [Al-Qaida leader] Osama bin Laden has told the Arabic satellite television station, al-Jazeerah, that he considers all male U.S. taxpayers to be legitimate targets—not that he had any qualms about the slaughter of women and presumably non-taxpayers at the World Trade Center in New York [that was a target of the September 11, 2001, terrorist attacks]. He also boasted to a visiting Saudi supporter, in the infamous home video, that he had "calculated in advance the number of casualties from the enemy." For bin Laden, Elaine Duch, the 49-year-old civilian office worker who suffered 77% burns, was an enemy casualty, not an innocent victim. Mullah Mohammed Omar, the leader of the Taliban, called for the destruction of America. If al-Qaida are soldiers, then so was Patty Hearst [a kidnapping victim who was pressured into helping her captors rob banks].

Detainees Are Dangerous Prisoners

To enjoy the rights of a POW, a combatant must not only stop fighting, he is explicitly forbidden from feigning surrender (article 37 of the 1977 First Additional Protocol). Clearly, the Taliban and al-Qaida fighters have not laid down their arms in the spirit intended by the Geneva Convention. To the best of their abilities, they have smuggled arms into prisons. Others have murdered their guards with anything that came to hand—one appears to have used his teeth. They surrender only to buy time, turning on their captors. . . . Some of the prisoners transported to Guantánamo Bay have vowed to continue murdering Americans, starting with the Marines looking after them. The U.S. has never had such dangerous prisoners before. At the end of the Second World War, German prisoners, many of whom had behaved with unparalleled viciousness until the last minute of hostilities, posed little threat to Allied troops after their surrender. Disillusioned Japanese officers took their own lives after the September 1945 surrender, but despite their earlier kamikaze tactics did not attempt to take Americans with them.

Even by the loosest definition, the detainees do not fit the Geneva Convention's conception of soldiers, militiamen or resistance fighters. Rather, they are in many ways a cross between spies, who clandestinely gather information, and pirates, who ignore civilized rules of conflict in the pursuit of loot. Indeed, bin Laden issued a 1996 statement that Americans' "wealth is a booty [prize] to those who kill them."

Strict Definitions Keep Everyone Safe

In previous wars, armies have treated men like those now in Camp X-Ray very harshly. During the nineteenth and early twentieth centuries, when warfare was by later standards restrained, such unlawful combatants were summarily executed. Napoleon's armies hanged and shot unlawful combatants, especially the Spanish guerrillas. The Prussians shot unlawful French combatants in 1871. The invading German army shot Belgians who were alleged to have been unlawful combatants in

1914, behavior that was reviled not because it was believed that unlawful combatants deserved to be spared, but because the Belgians had been carrying arms openly and wearing uniforms.

Maintaining a strict distinction between lawful combatants (conscripts, professionals, militiamen and resistance fighters) and unlawful combatants (such as bandits and terrorists) not only protects the dignity of real soldiers, it safeguards civilians. By defining who can be subject to violence and capture, the horror of war is, hopefully, focused away from civilians and limited to those willing to put themselves in the line of fire, and seek no cover other than that acquired by military skill.

> *Even by the loosest definition, the detainees do not fit the Geneva Convention's conception of soldiers, militiamen or resistance fighters.*

If we want soldiers to respect the lives of civilians and POWs, soldiers must be confident that civilians and prisoners will not attempt to kill them. Civilians who abuse their non-combatant status are a threat not only to soldiers who abide by the rules, they endanger innocents everywhere by drastically eroding the legal and customary restraints on killing civilians. Restricting the use of arms to lawful combatants has been a way of limiting war's savagery since at least the Middle Ages.

A Promotion from Mere Box-Cutters

Some critics of the Bush administration concede that al-Qaida and Taliban prisoners may not be entitled to POW status, but argue that this should be granted out of prudence. They claim that unless a uniform standard of behavior is maintained, we will not be able to protest against the abuse of American POWs in the future. Remarkably, we have been told that the Geneva Convention protected American captives in Vietnam and Korea, an assertion which surviving American POWs, such as Senator John McCain [whose Vietnamese captors mistreated him], will regard as a bad joke. Worse yet, if we set the precedent that we will give our foes the protections of the Geneva Convention no matter how badly they treat American soldiers and civilians, they will have no incentive to treat their American prisoners humanely. . . .

Others, such as Nicholas Kristof, a *New York Times* columnist, argue that legal generosity can do no harm. They feel that it does not matter that under article 17 of the Geneva Convention, a POW need only give "his surname, first name and rank, date of birth, and army, regimental, personal or serial number, or failing this, equivalent information." After all, argues Kristof: "we can still ask them anything we want to. In any case, detainees can't be forced to speak. The only practical way to facilitate interrogation would be to bring out thumbscrews."

Actually, experts on interrogation, unlike journalists, do not even consider torture a proper or useful means of obtaining information. Tortured detainees tell their captors what they want to hear, not the truths they need to know. Instead, as happened during the Second World War when the British were dealing with Nazi spies (who in 1942 were as highly motivated as al-Qaida members are in 2002), subtle psychological pressure can be used to great effect, as can the prospect of reduced terms of imprisonment. Under the convention, however, the detaining power is not permitted to give cooperative POWs preferential treatment over uncooperative POWs.

> *If we want soldiers to respect the lives of civilians and POWs, soldiers must be confident that civilians and prisoners will not attempt to kill them.*

Indeed, the Geneva Convention, assuming that prisoners are real soldiers, allows them to retain knives, which for al-Qaida is a promotion from mere box-cutters.[4] Under article 18: "Effects and articles used for their clothing or feeding shall likewise remain in their possession, even if such effects and articles belong to their regulation military equipment." POWs also have access to kitchen implements, innocent in most hands, but deadly when preparing Taliban cuisine, thanks to article 26: "Prisoners of war shall, as far as possible, be associated with the preparation of their meals; they may be employed for that purpose in the

---

4. The September 11, 2001, hijackers smuggled box-cutters aboard planes, and then used them as weapons to overwhelm passengers and crew.

kitchens. Furthermore, they shall be given the means of preparing, themselves, the additional food in their possession."

Granting POW Status Is Disastrous

American treatment of the al-Qaida and Taliban detainees has been, by any measure, more than humane. The three men confirmed as British subjects at Camp X-Ray have said that they have "no complaints" about their treatment. What the critics cannot grasp is that it is precisely because the U.S. takes its legal obligations seriously that it is being so careful with its captives—both in their treatment and with their status.

> *It is precisely because the U.S. takes its legal obligations seriously that it is being so careful with its captives—both in their treatment and with their status.*

In addition to the legal and military practicalities, there is an obvious moral danger in setting the precedent that captured terrorists are soldiers. Not only does that elevate [September 11th hijacker] Mohammad Atta from a calculating murderer into a combatant, it puts the [terrorist groups] IRA, ETA and the Red Brigades on a par with [legitimate armies such as] the Marine Corps and the French Resistance.

Clearly, al-Qaida and Taliban are part of an ongoing terrorist conspiracy, and need to be questioned. Al-Qaida's loose structure may mean that few individual members will have much information, but many will have lots of seemingly uninteresting scraps to tell, which properly collated and analyzed could be of immense value. Until they are interrogated, we will not know.

Remarkably, some human rights activists not only understand the restrictions that would be placed on POW interrogations, they seem to welcome them as a way of preventing information gathering. "If they are prisoners of war, there are restrictions on how they can be interrogated," acknowledged William F. Schulz, executive director of Amnesty International U.S.A. "POW's are required to provide only name, rank and serial number. If these POW's were in U.S. territory and were being interrogated about a war crime, they would have the right to an attorney. The fact that they are in Cuba makes that question ambiguous."

The implication of that statement is that the detainees should be given not just the protections of POWs, but also the safeguards of U.S. domestic criminal procedure. But the criminal courts are not the place to fight a war against an international organization researching nuclear weapons for use against American cities. If al-Qaida members are treated as criminals, and know their rights, under American law they can be questioned only in the presence of legal counsel, who would be professionally obliged to advise their clients to say nothing at all. The impact on intelligence gathering would be disastrous. . . .

To give the detainees a status they do not deserve, and protections that would both give aid and comfort to terrorists running free, would not only set a dangerous precedent. It would in the long run demolish the Geneva Convention and undermine the safety of American soldiers and civilians alike.

Empty Criticisms from America's Enemies

It is a curious irony that many of the voices calling for the U.S. to impose upon itself the most restrictive interpretations of the Geneva Convention, come from European nations that have not taken the same position when their own national interests were at stake.

> **"**Critics who term the transport of the detainees torture should ask themselves under what conditions, if any, they would board an aircraft with al-Qaida members?**"**

Of course, for some critics—not all of them European— Camp X-Ray is an opportunity to express their disappointment that Afghanistan was not the quagmire for America that they had hoped for. Their regret at the massacres of September 11th was shallow, as they demonstrated when arguing, explicitly or implicitly, that the U.S. "had it coming." Their warnings that the Taliban would prove invincible were proved wrong. They predicted that the war would cause a famine—instead, the U.S. and Afghan victory has helped alleviate hunger. Nor, to their dismay, has the so-called "Arab Street" [that is, Arab popular opinion] risen up as one in support of bin Laden. The first pictures [of the Cuba detainees], of men shackled and restrained, were, for these critics, evidence at long last of grievous and indisputable U.S. misconduct. That the pictures were released by the Pentagon, which would surely have no interest in giving such an impression, was ignored.

> *The Camp X-Ray inmates . . . know that it is far more pleasant to be an 'unlawful combatant' in U.S. custody than to be a POW almost anywhere else in the world.*

Being flown around in goggles and shackles is undoubtedly unpleasant, but al-Qaida has a certain record of behavior on aircraft. Critics who term the transport of the detainees torture should ask themselves under what conditions, if any, they would board an aircraft with al-Qaida members? Despite charges that the shackles, goggles and face masks constituted sensory deprivation, the detainees are not being treated in this way to "soften them up" [that is, torture them] for interrogation. The goggles and masks were removed after transport.

The U.S. Has High Standards of Prisoner Treatment

Incredibly, one leading British journalist contrasted "the continental ethic of human rights" with the supposedly weaker standard in the U.S. The problem is that European high standards rarely seem to translate into practice. The French socialist government sent secret service agents to blow up a Greenpeace vessel at anchor in New Zealand in 1985. The Spanish socialist government used counter-terror death squads, the Grupos Antiterroristas de Liberación (GAL) in the 1980s to kill Basque terrorists and, in some cases, innocent Basques. In Italy, state organs were involved in helping far-right terrorists. The record in Greece on terrorist detainees is perfect, for the simple reason that the Greek government has contrived never to arrest a single domestic terrorist, while releasing one foreign terrorist as a "freedom fighter."

Some critics claim that Camp X-Ray will undermine the U.S. position in Muslim countries. On January 21 [2002], just as writers were penning their denunciations of Camp X-Ray, Iran released 697 POWs held since the Iran-Iraq war of 1980–1988—despite the Geneva Convention's rule on releasing POWs immediately at the conclusion of a conflict. Syria has routinely murdered Israeli POWs. Iraq abused and tortured American and British POWs. In Afghanistan, fighters are either treated with excessive generosity, bribed to defect and then allowed to take their [guns] home with them, or subject to the grisliest ends, for example put into empty goods containers to suffocate to death.

> *The U.S. is rightly refusing to grant rights to those who clearly fail to qualify for them.*

Of course, most Camp X-Ray detainees are from Saudi Arabia, where dissidents who cannot be appeased are tortured or thrown from helicopters in the desert. The Camp X-Ray inmates seem to have few complaints because they, better than most, know that it is far more pleasant to be an "unlawful combatant" in U.S. custody than to be a POW almost anywhere else in the world.

The U.S. Respects the Geneva Convention

The United States is not leading a war between angels and demons. Rather, this is a conflict between imperfect, but freedom-loving democratic peoples, and demons—enemies who seek neither concessions, nor compromise, but the slaughter of Americans, with civilians preferred as targets to soldiers.

In this war, America has few real allies. While there are many who will express sympathy for America's losses, relatively few will stand up for America's right to defend itself aggressively—to do what must be done to protect its citizens from being international mass murderers.

The U.S. is trying hard to find the most humane way to wage, and win, this war. There is no precedent for this challenge and no perfect legal model that can be taken off the shelf. Yet it is precisely because the U.S. takes the Geneva Convention seriously, with both its protections for combatants and the line it draws between combatants and civilians, that the U.S. is being so careful in the use of the POW label. Some of the detainees may yet be termed POWs, but restricting the Geneva Convention's protections to those who obey its rules is the only mechanism that can make the Geneva Convention enforceable.

Supreme Court Justice Robert Jackson once said that the U.S. Constitution is not a suicide pact. Neither is the Geneva Convention. If well-meaning but misguided human rights activists turn the Geneva Convention into a terrorist's charter and a civilian's death warrant, the result will be that it will be universally ignored, with all that implies for the future of the international rule of law.

For Americans, whose own soldiers have been routinely abused in captivity, POW status matters. In contrast to other nations—which concede POW status casually, and then maltreat POWs horribly—the U.S. is rightly refusing to grant rights to those who clearly fail to qualify for them. The U.S. is, nonetheless, treating these unlawful combatants humanely, despite the unforgivable crimes they have committed and the worse atrocities that they continue to plot.

Addendum

The U.S. now gives the prisoners the right to a hearing before a competent tribunal, a mechanism which is in compliance with article 5 of the 1949 Geneva Convention relative to the Treatment of Prisoners of War (hereafter "Geneva Convention)." This formal and structured process, which is right and proper, is an improvement on the previous policy of reviewing the cases of prisoners periodically. Prisoners now have the right to challenge their detention in the court-like setting specified by the Geneva Convention. Devising procedures that are both just and prudent for people who are neither traditional prisoners-of-war (POWs) nor traditional criminals has proved extremely difficult, the balance is still evolving, and at the time of writing the current system is still being vigorously debated and periodically revised.

We now have less confidence that prisoners in U.S. custody will not be abused, because they have been in both Iraq and Afghanistan. We now have reason to think that the U.S. may have kept in prison, for longer than was necessary, people who were no longer a security threat. The U.S. government can be justly criticized on both counts. We also know that some of those that the U.S. released have returned to the war to fight U.S. forces, which explains understandable U.S. caution on this matter. Abuse and torture of prisoners, whether by rogue guards or by military intelligence officers desperate for information, is wholly unacceptable and must be dealt with through swift and well publicized investigations and prosecutions. There are no explanations or equivocations that can excuse the abuse and torture of prisoners that became a scandal after it was revealed at Abu Ghreib prison in Iraq.

We remain convinced that many people did not and do not deserve POW status as defined by the Geneva Convention, for the reasons we noted in the article.

Fredric Smoler is a professor at Sarah Lawrence College. Andrew Apostolou is Director of Research at the Foundation for the Defense of Democracies.

13

Prisoners Taken During the War on Terror Should Be Tried by Military Tribunal

Ruth Wedgwood

Before becoming a professor of international law, Ruth Wedgwood was a federal prosecutor.

Military courts are the most appropriate place to prosecute detainees in the war on terror. Federal courts are not equipped to handle the kind of evidence that would be brought against terrorists. Furthermore, placing Americans on juries to judge terrorist trials could endanger their lives. International courts have proven to be costly, slow, and inefficient, and so are not ideal venues for prosecuting terrorists either. The president has the constitutional power to convene military tribunals and should be allowed to pursue this privilege without interference.

U.S. Marines may have to burrow down an Afghan cave to smoke out the leadership of [the terrorist group] al Qaeda. It would be ludicrous to ask that they pause in the dark to pull an Afghan-language Miranda card[1] from their kit bag. This is war, not a criminal case.

1. U.S. police officers must read Miranda rights to anyone being arrested for a crime. These include making sure the perpetrator understands that they have the right to remain silent, the right to refuse to answer questions, and the right to consult an attorney.

The president's executive order, providing for the detention and possible trial of terrorists in military courts, recognizes this. But some critics continue to argue that trials are better held in a federal district court, or in an ad hoc international criminal tribunal. Others have worried that the initial jurisdictional order does not fully specify the rules of trial procedure and evidence that would await prisoners. Yet others are concerned that Congress was not asked for authorizing legislation. These criticisms, though made in good faith, reflect a misunderstanding of how the law of war is enforced, as well as a dangerous naivete about the threat we face.

Military Courts Are the Best Place to Prosecute Terrorists

The detention of combatants is a traditional prerogative of war. We have all seen movies about captured soldiers in World War II. After surrender or capture, a soldier can be parked for the rest of the war, in humane conditions, to prevent him from returning to the fight. His detention does not depend on being charged with a crime. Though most al Qaeda members do not rise even to the level of POWs [prisoners of war]—they have trampled on the qualifying rules of wearing distinctive insignia and observing the laws of war—they can be detained by the same authority for the duration of the conflict.

> *These criticisms [of military courts], though made in good faith, reflect a misunderstanding of how the law of war is enforced, as well as a dangerous naivete about the threat we face.*

Military courts are the traditional venue for enforcing violations of the law of war. The murder of [three thousand] civilians [during the terrorist attacks of September 11, 2001] was an act of war, as recognized by the U.N. Security Council in two resolutions endorsing America's right to use force in self-defense. [Al Qaeda leader] Osama bin Laden and his airborne henchmen disregarded two fundamental principles of morality and law in war—never deliberately attack civilians, and never seek disproportionate damage to civilians in pursuit of another objective. The choice to carry out the attacks during the morning rush hour reveals this to be a war crime of historic magnitude.

Considering the Logistics

Why not try al Qaeda members in . . . federal courts, with a civilian judge and a jury? Federal judges have never been involved in the detention of POWs or unprivileged combatants. Only in 1996 did federal courts gain limited statutory jurisdiction to hear war crimes matters, and no federal court has ever heard such a case.

Moreover, just consider the logistics. It is hard to imagine assigning three carloads of federal marshals, rotated every two weeks, to protect each juror for the rest of his life. An al Qaeda member trained in surveillance can easily follow jurors home, even when their names are kept anonymous. Perhaps it is only coincidence that the World Trade Center towers toppled the day before al Qaeda defendants were due to be sentenced for the earlier bombings of East Africa embassies—in a federal courthouse in lower Manhattan six blocks away. But certainly before Sept. 11 no one imagined the gargantuan appetite for violence and revenge that bin Laden has since exhibited. Endangering America's cities with a repeat performance is a foolish act.

If there are a sizeable number of al Qaeda captures, the sheer volume will also be disabling. At a rate of (at most) 12 defendants per trial, trying 700 al Qaeda members would take upwards of 50 judges, sequestered in numerous courthouses around the country.

> *An al Qaeda member trained in surveillance can easily follow jurors home, even when their names are kept anonymous.*

In federal court, as well, there are severe limitations on what evidence can be heard by a jury. Hearsay statements of probative value, admissible in military commissions, European criminal courts, and international courts, cannot be considered in a trial by jury. Historically, Anglo-American juries were thought incapable of weighing out-of-court statements, and the Supreme

Court attached many of these jury rules to the Constitution. So bin Laden's telephone call to his mother, telling her that "something big" was imminent, could not be entered into evidence if the source of information was his mother's best friend. In a terrorist trial, there are few eyewitnesses willing to testify, because conspiracy cells are compartmentalized, and witnesses fear revenge.

> *This danger is too serious to be left to the civilian courts.*

There is also the problem of publishing information to the world, and to al Qaeda, through an open trial record. As [former British prime minister Winston] Churchill said, your enemy shouldn't know how you have penetrated his operations. The 1980 Classified Information Procedures Act helped to handle classified secrets at trial, but doesn't permit closing the trial or the protection of equally sensitive unclassified operational information.

International Courts Are Impractical

An international tribunal is even less practical. The ad hoc criminal tribunals created for [war crimes commited in] Yugoslavia and Rwanda by the U.N. Security Council have not enjoyed the confidence of Western powers in obtaining intelligence intercepts for use at trial. Americans could not expect to fill the majority of slots in an ad hoc tribunal, and a trial chamber of three to five judges might have no Americans at all. Moreover, the tribunal for Yugoslavia has operated at a snail's pace, trying only 31 defendants in eight years, at a cost of $400 million.

It is even more fanciful to propose that a largely Muslim court should be delegated to try bin Laden and company. Arab and Muslim states will fear the reaction of their own local militants. And Israel might properly wonder why it could not also serve on such an international court, since bin Laden's fatwa called for the murder of Jews and Americans. No Arab state would participate, of course, if an Israeli judge served. This does not preclude offering into evidence, at a military tribunal, the works of international law by Muslim jurists that show that the standards of protecting innocents are universal.

Congress will want to consult on the nature of the military tribunals established by President [George W.] Bush. Congress's input will be useful to the administration in crafting rules of procedure and evidence, as well as in thinking about added safeguards for alleged terrorists discovered within the U.S. Civilian judges can serve on military tribunals . . . and few hearings may be closed, except for sensitive portions. Habeas corpus review[2] remains available for aliens arrested in the U.S.

But it is also plain that Congress long ago agreed to the president's power to convene military commissions (under U.S. Code, Title 10, Section 821). In addition, the president has inherent constitutional power as commander-in-chief to convene such tribunals, an argument acknowledged by Chief Justice Harlan Fiske Stone in a 1942 opinion. (Stone, writing for a unanimous Supreme Court, declined to set aside the military trial and execution of German saboteurs who had entered the U.S. to destroy war plants.) The president is also authorized by statute to write rules of procedure and proof for military commissions, and to decide whether or not it is "practicable" to adopt the ordinary rules of common law and evidence.

The thought of printing stationery for the "United States district court for the district of Afghanistan" sounds rather absurd. And for good reason. This danger is too serious to be left to the civilian courts.

Note: Please see Ruth Wedgwood's June 28, 2004, *Wall Street Journal* op-ed "Law and Torture" for more information on the use of torture.

---

2. Habeas corpus is the process of bringing the accused before a court of law to determine, prior to a trial, if the person is being legally detained.

14

Prisoners Taken During the War on Terror Should Not Be Tried by Military Tribunal

Harold Hongju Koh

Harold Hongju Koh was the assistant secretary of state for democracy, human rights, and labor from 1998 to 2001. He currently teaches international law at Yale Law School.

U.S. courts, not military tribunals, are the best place to prosecute suspects in the war on terror. U.S. courts protect the rights of defendants, dispense universally accepted justice, and have repeatedly proven that they can effectively handle a variety of terrorism cases. Military tribunals, in contrast, fall short of the judicial norms that are treasured in America. They violate basic legal rights and are biased decision-making bodies. Moreover, verdicts dispensed by military tribunals are not considered credible in the eyes of the world, thereby undermining America's effort to lead an international campaign against terrorism. International courts are not appropriate venues either, as they are best used when there is no other competent court available.

[In January 2002], Zacarias Moussaoui, a French national of Moroccan descent, pleaded "not guilty" in Virginia federal court to six counts of conspiring to commit acts of international terrorism in connection with the September 11 [2001] attacks on the Pentagon and the World Trade Center. In other

Harold Hongju Koh, "Against Military Tribunals," *Dissent*, Fall 2002, pp. 58–62.

times, it would have seemed unremarkable for an American civilian court to try someone charged with conspiring to murder American citizens and destroy American property on American soil. . . . In recent decades, U.S. courts have decided criminal cases convicting international hijackers, terrorists, and drug smugglers, as well as a string of well-publicized civil lawsuits adjudicating gross human rights violations. Most pertinent, federal prosecutors have successfully tried and convicted in U.S. courts more than twenty-five members or affiliates of al-Qaeda, the very terrorist group now charged with planning the September 11 attacks, for earlier attacks on the World Trade Center and two U.S. embassies.[1]

This history made even more surprising President George W. Bush's military order of November 13, 2001, which, without congressional authorization or consultation, suddenly declared that "to protect the United States and its citizens, . . . *it is necessary for* [noncitizen suspects designated by the president under the order] . . . *to be tried for violations of the laws of war and other applicable laws by military tribunals."* (Emphasis added.) Bush's order has attracted harsh criticism abroad and milder challenge at home. Responding to this furor, regulations finally issued by the Defense Department in March [2002] now purport to guarantee some procedural protections to defendants brought before such military, commissions, but no right to judicial review before civilian judges.

> A military commission cannot be an independent court, and its commissioners are not genuinely independent decision makers.

Amid this controversy, the practical question remains: given the exigencies created by September 11, what's wrong with the U.S. government's trying suspected terrorists before military commissions? Bush's order is wrong for two simple reasons: first, it undermines the United States' perceived commitment to the rule of law and national judicial institutions at precisely the moment that commitment is most needed here at home. Sec-

---

1. The author is referring to the 1993 bombing of the World Trade Center, and the 1998 bombings of U.S. embassies in Kenya and Tanzania.

ond, by failing to deliver justice that the world at large will find credible, the military order undermines our ability to pursue our core post–September 11 aim: leading an international campaign against terrorism under a rule-of-law banner. . . .

Dispensing with Defendants' Rights

The order authorizes the Defense Department to dispense with the basic procedural guarantees required by the Bill of Rights, the International Covenant on Civil and Political Rights, and the Third Geneva Convention of 1949,[2] to which the United States is a party. To the extent that current Defense Department regulations now provide for these procedures, they could be changed tomorrow. And insofar as any of these guarantees— which include the presumption of innocence, the rights to be informed of charges and to equal treatment before the courts, public hearings, independent and impartial decision makers, the rights to speedy trial, confrontation of adverse witnesses, and counsel of one's own choosing, the privilege against self-incrimination, and review by a higher tribunal according to law—are subject to suspension in time of emergency, the Bush administration has taken no formal steps to declare an emergency (or to explain the need for such a declaration). . . . Under the order, the president directs his subordinates to create military commissions, to determine who shall be tried before them, and to choose the finders of fact, law, and guilt. However detailed its rules and procedures may be, a military commission cannot be an independent court, and its commissioners are not genuinely independent decision makers, but military officers who are ultimately answerable to the very secretary of defense and president who prosecute the cases before them. "Such blending of functions in one branch of the Government," Justice Hugo Black recognized, "is the objectionable thing which the draftsmen of the Constitution endeavored to prevent by providing for the separation of governmental powers."

Undermining the Rule of Law

If international law allows the United States to redress the unprovoked killing of thousands on September 11 by bombing al-Qaeda perpetrators [in the war on terror], what obliges the

2. These documents lay out basic, universal human rights.

United States to give captured accused culprits any trial at all? The answer to this question addresses the most fundamental rule-of-law concerns. Trials promote four legal values that are higher than vengeance: holding the perpetrators accountable for their crimes against humanity; telling the world the truth about those crimes; reaffirming the norms of civilized society; and demonstrating that law-abiding societies, unlike terrorists, respect human rights by channeling retribution into criminal punishment for even the most heinous outlaws. The military order undermines each of these values.

First, military commissions create the impression of kangaroo courts, not legitimate mechanisms of accountability. Second, rather than openly announcing the truth, commissions tend to hide the very facts and principles the United States now seeks to announce to the world. Third, because military tribunals in Burma, Colombia, Egypt, Peru, Turkey, and elsewhere have been perceived as granting judgments based on politics, not legal norms, the U.S. Department of State has regularly pressed to have cases involving U.S. citizens heard in civilian courts in those countries.

> *Supporters of military commissions have mistakenly concluded that standing American courts are somehow incapable of rendering full, fair, and expeditious justice.*

Perversely, the military order threatens national confidence in existing legal institutions just when that confidence is already badly shaken by horrific terrorist attacks. Despite those attacks, both the presidency and Congress have continued to function, yet the order implicitly assumes that the third branch, comprising existing civilian and military courts, can no longer handle the very cases it dealt with just days before the attacks occurred. Supporters of military commissions have mistakenly concluded that standing American courts are somehow incapable of rendering full, fair, and expeditious justice in such cases. One might understand resorting to a military commission in a country where no currently functioning court could fairly and efficiently try the case. But over the centuries, the U.S. judicial system has amply demonstrated its ability to adapt to new, complex problems in criminal and civil law. Why should the United States try suspects in military commissions that fall short of the judicial norms to which we are committed, when our own federal courts have repeatedly and fairly tried al-Qaeda members?

> ❝ *Military commissions provide ad hoc justice and hence uncertain protection for defendants' rights.* ❞

Finally, military commissions provide ad hoc justice and hence uncertain protection for defendants' rights. Although the Defense Department's regulations now offer greater protections for the accused, those regulations—unlike the Bill of Rights, the Federal Rules of Criminal Procedure, or the Uniform Code of Military Justice—cannot guarantee those rights, as they are subject to change at the president's will. . . .

Undermining America's Moral Leadership

Using military commissions harms our strategic interests. The tactic potentially endangers Americans overseas by undermining the U.S. government's ability to protest effectively when other countries use such tribunals. Most important, espousing military commissions undermines U.S. moral leadership abroad. The United States regularly takes other countries to task for military proceedings that violate basic civil rights. How, then, can the United States be surprised when its European allies refuse to extradite captured terrorist suspects to U.S. military justice? When the Chinese or Russians try Uighur or Chechen Muslims as terrorists in military courts, U.S. diplomats protest vigorously, and the world condemns those tribunals as anti-Muslim. We can hardly object when other countries choose to treat U.S. military commissions the same way.

The Bush administration has missed the key point: to win a global war against terrorism, nations that claim moral rectitude and fidelity to the rule of law must not only apply, but universally be seen to be applying, credible justice. Credible justice for international crimes demands tribunals that are fair and impartial *both in fact and in appearance.* By their very nature, military tribunals fail this test. Through extensive tinkering, the Defense Department's regulations have now sought to ensure that any military commissions convened will operate more fairly in fact. Even if such a result could be ensured, the commission's judgments will never be perceived as fair by those skeptical of their political purpose, namely, the very Muslim nations whose continuing support the United States needs to maintain its coalition against terrorism. The Defense Department will end up chasing its own tail. The more the department tries to address the perceived unfairness of military tribunals by making them more "court-like"—more transparent, with more procedural protections, and more independent decision makers—the more these modifications will eliminate the supposed "practical" advantages of having military tribunals in the first place, and still not dispel the fatal global perception of unfairness.

Other Options?

Did we have other options? How should the United States have pursued the issue of justice after September 11? To ensure that the international community perceived that those convicted for the September 11 attacks would receive fair and impartial justice, the United States should . . . bring suspects only before standing tribunals that have demonstrated their capacity to dispense such justice in the past.

> *Sweeping all 'unlawful combatants' who have committed 'war crimes' into untested, unwise, and legally deficient U.S. military commissions is a short-sighted strategy.*

Soon after September 11, some people argued that we should press for a new international tribunal to try terrorists. Given the administration's hostility to the International Criminal Court, that proposal never received serious political consideration. Although I have long supported international adjudication, I am skeptical about the international community's ability to overcome existing political obstacles and to create a fair tribunal quickly. International tribunals make the most sense when there is no functioning municipal court that could fairly and efficiently try the case, as happened in the former Yugoslavia and Rwanda. But even if the U.S. government were to support such a tribunal, . . . recent history shows that building new international tribunals from scratch is slow and expensive and requires arduous negotiations. Although proponents claim that an international tribunal would be more likely than a U.S. court to be viewed as impartial, an ad hoc tribunal created for the express purpose of trying the September 11 terrorists would not find greater acceptance in the Muslim world than the judgments of a civilian court system that has been in place for more than two centuries. . . .

U.S. Courts Can Dispense Universal Justice

[Therefore,] the United States should [send] for trial before American civilian courts by seasoned federal prosecutors only those cases involving defendants (such as leading al-Qaeda members) who have been charged with or suspected of murdering or plotting to murder American citizens on American soil. Since three al-Qaeda suspects—Zacarias Moussaoui, the "American Taliban" John Walker Lindh (who has now accepted a plea bargain), and the "shoe bomber," Richard Reid[3]—have been brought before U.S. civilian courts, I see no need to charge any future defendants before untested and suspect military commissions. (Indeed, John Walker Lindh's plea bargain only demonstrated again that the existing criminal justice process is fully capable of handling even trials of detainees whose crime was fighting alongside the Taliban.)

Instead, our government now holds hundreds on Guantánamo [Bay, Cuba, the site of a U.S. military detention center], and may initiate military commissions there. Two American citizens—Yasser Hamdi and José Padilla—are being held as "enemy combatants"—incommunicado and without due process[4]—in military facilities within the United States. Although fellow Americans John Walker Lindh and confessed mass murderer Timothy McVeigh [a terrorist who blew up a federal building in Oklahoma in 1995] enjoyed full legal rights and representation throughout their proceedings, these other Americans are being denied all procedural rights. Yet sweeping all "unlawful combat-

3. On December 22, 2001, al-Qaeda operative Richard Reid tried to blow up a transatlantic flight by hiding explosives in his shoes. 4. a term referring to fundamental legal rights, such as the right to be heard, the right to a fair trial, and the right to an impartial jury

ants" who have committed "war crimes" into untested, unwise, and legally deficient U.S. military commissions is a short-sighted strategy that will surely invite hostile foreign governments reciprocally to "try" and execute captured nonuniformed American personnel before similar tribunals.

In sum, the battle against global terrorism requires credible justice, which military commissions cannot provide. Credible international tribunals can provide credible justice but would be difficult to create under the current political circumstances. That leaves standing civilian courts or courts-martial that operate under preexisting and transparent rules. Creating military commissions, using Guantánamo, and labeling American criminal defendants as "enemy combatants" have been tragic and unnecessary errors. If the United States wants to show the world its commitment to the very rule of law that the terrorists sought to undermine, it should take this opportunity to demonstrate that American courts can give universal justice.

Organizations to Contact

The editors have compiled the following list of organizations concerned with the issues debated in this book. The descriptions are derived from materials provided by the organizations. All have publications or information available for interested readers. The list was compiled on the date of publication of the present volume; the information provided here may change. Be aware that many organizations take several weeks or longer to respond to inquiries, so allow as much time as possible.

American Civil Liberties Union (ACLU)
125 Broad St., 18th Fl., New York, NY 10004-2400
(888) 567-ACLU
e-mail: aclu@aclu.org • Web site: www.aclu.org

Founded in 1920, the ACLU is a national organization that works to defend civil liberties in the United States. It publishes various materials on the Bill of Rights, including regular in-depth reports, the triannual newsletter *Civil Liberties*, and a set of handbooks on individual rights.

Amnesty International (AI)
322 Eighth Ave., New York, NY 10001
(212) 807-8400 • fax: (212) 463-9193
e-mail: admin-us@aiusa.org • Web site: www.amnesty.org

Made up of over 1.8 million members in over 150 countries, AI is dedicated to promoting human rights worldwide. Since its inception in 1961, the organization has focused much of its effort on the eradication of torture. AI maintains an extremely active news Web site, distributes a large annual report on the state of human rights in every country (as well as numerous special reports on specific human rights issues), and publishes the *Wire*, the monthly magazine of AI.

Association for the Prevention of Torture (APT)
Route de Ferney 10, Case Postale 2267, 1211 Genéve 2, Switzerland
+41 (22) 919 2170 • fax: +41 (22) 919 2180
e-mail: apt@apt.ch • Web site: www.apt.ch

Hosted in Geneva, Switzerland, the APT actively works to end torture worldwide. It publishes the *APT Newsletter* three times per year, maintains a detailed annual report on torture around the world, and prints specific manuals and special reports detailing specific issues and events pertaining to torture.

The Brookings Institution
1775 Massachusetts Ave. NW, Washington, DC 20036
(202) 797-6000 • fax: (202) 797-6004
e-mail: brookinfo@brook.edu • Web site: www.brookings.org

The institution, founded in 1927, is a think tank that conducts research and education in foreign policy, economics, government, and the social sciences. In 2001 it began America's Response to Terrorism, a project that provides briefings and analysis to the public and which is featured on the center's Web site. Other publications include the quarterly *Brookings Review*, periodic *Policy Briefs*, and books including *Terrorism and U.S. Foreign Policy*.

Center for Strategic and International Studies (CSIS)
1800 K St. NW, Suite 400, Washington, DC 20006
(202) 887-0200 • fax: (202) 775-3199
Web site: www.csis.org

The center works to provide world leaders with strategic insights and policy options on current and emerging global issues. It publishes books including *To Prevail: An American Strategy for the Campaign Against Terrorism;* the *Washington Quarterly*, a journal on political, economic, and security issues; and other publications including reports that can be downloaded from its Web site.

Department of Homeland Security (DHS)
Washington, DC 20528
Web site: www.dhs.gov

The Department of Homeland Security was created in direct response to the terrorist attacks of September 11, 2001. It was the largest reshaping of the federal government since 1949. With this change, many formerly disparate offices became united in a mission to prevent terrorist attacks on American soil, reduce the country's vulnerability to terrorism, and effectively respond to attacks that did occur. The Department of Homeland Security took branches formerly of the Departments of Treasury, Justice, Agriculture, Energy, Commerce, Transportation, and Defense under its extensive wing. Services from the Coast Guard to Customs are now linked under the same umbrella, all with the singular mission of protecting the United States from attack.

European Committee for the Prevention of Torture and Inhuman or Degrading Treatment or Punishment (CPT)
Human Rights Building, Council of Europe
F-67075 Strasbourg Cedex, France
+33 (3) 8841 3939 • fax: +33 (3) 8841 2772
e-mail: cptdoc@coe.int • Web site: www.cpt.coe.int

The CPT originated with the 1987 passage of the European Convention for the Prevention of Torture and Inhuman or Degrading Treatment or Punishment, an international treaty ratified by forty-five members of the European Council. The CPT performs site visits in participating countries to ensure that no torture or other inhuman treatment is taking place. It maintains a large online database detailing torture reports and site visits, and publishes numerous reports, standards, and reference documents pertaining to torture.

Human Rights Watch (HRW)
350 Fifth Ave., 34th Fl., New York, NY 10118-3299
(212) 290-4700 • fax: (212) 736-1300
e-mail: hrwnyc@hrw.org • Web site: www.hrw.org

In 1988 several large regional organizations dedicated to promoting human rights merged to form HRW, a global watchdog group. HRW publishes numerous books, policy papers, and special reports (including a comprehensive annual report), sponsors an annual film festival on human rights issues, and files lawsuits on behalf of those whose rights are violated.

International Committee of the Red Cross (ICRC)
Washington, D.C., Regional Delegation
2100 Pennsylvania Ave. NW, Suite 545, Washington, DC 20037
(202) 293-9430 • fax: (202) 293-9431
e-mail: washington.was@icrc.org • Web site: www.icrc.org

Founded in 1863, the ICRC is one of the few organizations to have won the Nobel Peace Prize (and did so on three occasions: in 1917, 1944, and 1963). It was the ICRC that led to the creation of the Geneva Conventions on the treatment of prisoners of war, the wounded, and medical personnel, among others. Today, the ICRC continues its mission by investigating reports of human rights violations, assisting in disaster relief, and working on behalf of those who are wounded or imprisoned in wartime.

International Policy Institute of Counter-Terrorism (ICT)
PO Box 167, Herzlia 46150, Israel
972-9-9527277 • fax: 972-9-9513073
e-mail: mail@ict.org.il • Web site: www.ict.org.il

ICT is a research institute dedicated to developing public policy solutions to international terrorism. The ICT Web site is a comprehensive resource on terrorism and counterterrorism, featuring an extensive database on terrorist attacks and organizations, including al Qaeda.

U.S. Department of Justice (USDOJ)
950 Pennsylvania Ave. NW, Washington, DC 20530-0001
(202) 514-2000
e-mail: askdoj@usdoj.gov • Web site: www.usdoj.gov

The U.S. Department of Justice is responsible for enforcing U.S. federal law, and assisting local and international law enforcement efforts as needed. The official USDOJ Web site features numerous special reports, a "Kids' Page," and a frequently updated news site.

U.S. Department of State, Counterterrorism Office
Office of Public Affairs, Room 2507
2201 C St. NW, Washington, DC 20520
(202) 647-6575
e-mail: secretary@state.gov • Web site: www.state.gov/s/ct

The U.S. Department of State's counterterrorism office is responsible for coordinating international efforts to fight terrorism. The office's Web site includes pages dealing with current events, patterns of global terrorism, homeland security, and other issues pertaining to counterterrorism efforts.

World Organization Against Torture (OMCT)
Organisation Mondiale Contre la Torture International Secretariat, PO Box 21, 8, Rue du Vieux-Billard, CH-1211 Geneva 8, Switzerland
+41 (22) 809 4939 • fax: +41 (22) 809 4929
e-mail: omct@omct.org • Web site: www.omct.org

The OMCT is a global network of three hundred organizations dedicated to fighting torture and other forms of violence. It initiates numerous campaigns that assist victims of torture, promote the rights of children, monitor police activity, and take other measures designed to combat torture. OMCT maintains a large news archive and publishes many special reports on torture and violence.

Bibliography

Books

Amnesty International — *United States of America—the Threat of a Bad Example: Undermining International Standards as "War on Terror" Detentions Continue.* London: International Secretariat, 2003.

Reed Brody — *The Road to Abu Ghraib.* New York: Human Rights Watch, 2004.

Cynthia Brown — *Lost Liberties: Ashcroft and the Assault on Personal Freedom.* New York: New Press, 2003.

Richard A. Clarke — *Against All Enemies: Inside America's War on Terror.* New York: Free Press, 2004.

John Conroy — *Unspeakable Acts, Ordinary People: The Dynamics of Torture.* Berkeley: University of California Press, 2001.

Mark Danner — *Torture and Truth: America, Abu Ghraib, and the War on Terror.* New York: New York Review Books, 2004.

Alan M. Dershowitz — *America on Trial: Inside the Legal Battles That Transformed Our Nation—from the Salem Witches to the Guantanamo Detainees.* New York: Warner Books, 2004.

Seymour M. Hersh — *Chain of Command: The Road from 9/11 to Abu Ghraib.* New York: HarperCollins, 2004.

Michael Ignatieff — *The Lesser Evil: Political Ethics in an Age of Terror.* Princeton, NJ: Princeton University Press, 2004.

Chalmers Johnson — *The Sorrows of Empire: Militarism, Secrecy, and the End of the Republic [The American Empire Project].* New York: Metropolitan Books, 2004.

Charles W. Kegley Jr. — *The New Global Terrorism: Characteristics, Causes, Controls.* Upper Saddle River, NJ: Prentice-Hall, 2002.

Bernard Lewis — *The Crisis of Islam: Holy War and Unholy Terror.* Waterville, ME: Thorndike Press, 2003.

Gus Martin — *Understanding Terrorism: Challenges, Perspectives, and Issues.* Thousand Oaks, CA: Sage, 2003.

Michael Ratner — *America's Disappeared: Secret Imprisonment, Detainees, and the "War on Terror."* New York: Seven Stories, 2004.

Michael Ratner and Ellen Ray	*Guantanamo: What the World Should Know.* White River Junction, VT: Chelsea Green, 2004.
David Rose	*Guantanamo: The War on Human Rights.* New York: New Press, 2004.
Pamela M. Von Ness	*Guantanamo Bay Detainees: National Security or Civil Liberty?* Carlisle Barracks, PA: U.S. Army War College, 2003.

Periodicals

Gordon Bishop	"America Owes No Apologies for Fighting Terrorists," *EtherZone.com*, May 19, 2004.
Mark Bowden	"The Dark Art of Interrogation," *Atlantic Monthly*, October 2003.
Lincoln Caplan	"War's Conventions," *Legal Affairs*, July/August 2004.
Tom Englehardt	"Welcome to Guantanamo World," *Alternet.org*, April 5, 2004.
Thomas Fleming	"Loyal Opposition," *Chronicles*, August 2003.
Ilana Freedman	"Another Look at Abu Ghraib," *Metro West Daily News*, June 18, 2004.
Nancy Gibbs	"Their Humiliation, and Ours," *Time*, May 17, 2004.
Jonah Goldberg	"The World According to Me: Why Torture Is Sometimes Good, and Democracy Is Bad," *National Review*, October 12, 2001.
Scott Higham, Joe Stephens, and Margot Williams	"Guantanamo—a Holding Cell in War on Terror," *Washington Post*, May 2, 2004.
Henry Mark Holzer	"In Defense of Torture," *FrontPageMagazine.com*, November 29, 2002.
Nicholas M. Horrock and Anwar Iqbal	"Waiting for Gitmo," *Mother Jones*, January/February 2004.
Tom Malinowski	"The Logic of Torture," *Washington Post*, June 27, 2004.
Elisa Massimino	"Alien Justice: What's Wrong with Military Trials of Terrorist Suspects?" *Human Rights*, Winter 2002.
George Monbiot	"One Rule for Them . . . ," *Alternet.org*, March 26, 2003.
Kate O'Beirne	"It's a War, Stupid: Understanding and Misunderstanding the Detainees," *National Review*, September 16, 2002.
Alasdair Palmer	"The U.S. May Use Torture Against Terrorism," *Daily Telegraph*, December 15, 2002.

Eyal Press — "In Torture We Trust?" *Nation*, March 31, 2003.

Jeremy Rabkin — "After Guantanamo: The War over the Geneva Convention," *National Interest*, Summer 2002.

Chitra Ragavan and Carol Hook — "Law in a New Sort of War," *U.S. News & World Report*, April 26, 2004.

Amanda Ripley — "The Rules of Interrogation: It's a Murky Business, but Some Methods Work Better than Others," *Time*, May 17, 2004.

Bruce Shapiro — "POWs in Legal Limbo," *Nation*, February 25, 2002.

Harvey A. Silverglate — "Torture Warrants?" *Boston Phoenix*, December 6, 2001.

Alisa Solomon — "The Case Against Torture," *Village Voice*, December 4, 2001.

David Tell — "Civil Hysteria," *Weekly Standard*, July 29, 2002.

Jonathan Turley — "Appetite for Authoritarianism Spawns an American Gulag," *Los Angeles Times*, May 2, 2003.

Index